GERMAN SHEPHERD

FROM THE EDITORS OF DOGFANCY. MAGAZINE

CONTENTS

German Shepherd Dog, a Smart Owner's Guide®
part of the Kennel Club Books® Interactive Series®
ISBN: 978-1-593787-46-2. ©2009

Kennel Club Books Inc., 40 Broad St., Freehold, NJ 07728. Printed in Canada.
All rights reserved. No part of this book may be reproduced in any form,
by Photostat, scanner, microfilm, xerography or any other means, or incorporated
into any information retrieval system, electronic or mechanical,
without the written permission of the copyright owner.

*photographers include Isabelle Francias/BowTie Inc.; Tara Darling/BowTie Inc.;
Gina Cioli and Pamela Hunnicutt/BowTie Inc. Contributing writer: Susan Samms*

For CIP information, see page 176.
14 13 12 11   2 3 4 5 6 7 8 9 10

K9 EXPERT

So, you have a German Shepherd Dog or are thinking about getting one. Excellent! You have chosen a fabulous breed. For years to come, your GSD will be your best pal, protect your property and love your kids.

German Shepherds have long been used as protection, police and bomb-sniffing dogs. But they've been companions to man — mainly shepherds — for much longer. Their herding instinct remains strong today. If you have children, livestock or even geese, your new friend will want to "herd" them whenever he gets a chance. This can be great if your toddler is wandering toward the street, or a problem if you have fowl on your property who don't really need a dog ordering them around!

For whatever reason you've chosen a German Shepherd from the many dog breeds available, he's sure to fit the bill. A GSD will be happy to jog with you once he's full-grown, patrol the perimeter of your property each morning and take an agility class, too.

This breed is highly trainable, wanting to learn whatever it is you want to teach. So, if you want to try flyball, compete in schutzhund events, do therapy work at a hospital or even give the show dog world a whirl, you've selected the right breed.

However, it's not all about what your new friend can do for you. You've chosen a breed that craves attention and affection. Months spent in pastures, with just one human companion, over generations and generations, has created a dog who tightly latches on to his master. This means you can't put him in the backyard to fend for himself or expect him to be happy spending 10 hours a day in a crate.

You'll need to walk him each morning and night, spend time playing with him every day, let him sit next to you for lots of petting and also find a way to expend his mighty energy. That could translate to regular dog park visits, agility classes or a nightly jog. Whatever you choose, your GSD won't see this as a necessary "trip to the gym," but as his chance to be with you. And he'll keep watch over you the whole time.

Another great thing about this breed is its ease with other pets. Most GSDs get along just fine with the family cat, other dogs and even smaller pets. Because they're herders, not ratters, they don't have the need to pounce on hamsters and guinea pigs like terriers and some other breeds do. Supervision is required, of course, but you won't have a prey-starved dog on your hands.

If you've never had the good fortune to live with a German Shepherd before, you'll be surprised at his versatility. With consistent training and patient assistance, this

JOIN OUR ONLINE Club GSD®

With this Smart Owner's Guide®, you are well on your way to getting your GSD diploma. But your German Shepherd Dog education doesn't end here. You're invited to join **Club GSD®** (**DogChannel.com/Club-GSD**), a FREE online site with lots of fun and instructive features such as:

◆ **forums, blogs** and **profiles** where you can connect with other GSD owners
◆ **downloadable charts** and **checklists** to help you be a smart and loving GSD owner
◆ access to GSD **e-cards** and **wallpapers**
◆ interactive **games**
◆ canine **quizzes**

The **Smart Owner's Guide®** series and **Club GSD®** are backed by the experts at DOG FANCY® magazine and DogChannel.com — who have been providing trusted and up-to-date information about dogs and dog people for more than 40 years. Log on and join the club today!

dog can accomplish anything. And if you just want a super canine friend, a GSD will, of course, be just that. Be a super human friend to him, and you'll be a contented pair for many years to come. Enjoy your new friend. He'll never let you down.

Susan Chaney
Editor, DOG FANCY

ENGINEERING

Without question, the German Shepherd Dog's temperament and intelligence have earned him an international fan club. His affable, easygoing nature gives way to a strong protective instinct when provoked. People close to the breed frequently claim that German Shepherd Dogs know right from wrong and that a well-trained GSD is the best roommate you could ask for. The breed standard (a written description of the ideal GSD) refers to aloofness and self-confidence "that does not lend itself to immediate and indiscriminate friendships ... The ideal [German Shepherd Dog] is a working animal with an incorruptible character combined with a body and gait suitable for the arduous work that constitutes his primary purpose."

The traits of keen intelligence and trainability have made the German Shepherd Dog arguably the most versatile breed in the history of dogdom. In addition to their traditional roles as police and herding dogs, the breed excels at tracking, rescue, service work, obedience, agility, home sentry and scent identification.

> it's a
> **Fact**
>
> **The first dog to guide a blind person was a German Shepherd named Buddy in 1929.** Today, The Seeing Eye® foundation — the first organization to train guide dogs for the visually impaired — still counts on this breed, among others, to carry out its mission.

PERSONALITY POINTS

Throughout history, in whatever capacity the German Shepherd has been used, one thing that has remained constant is the bond between the dogs and their owners. Because GSDs have traditionally been used as service and working dogs, this bond was a necessity. Shepherds had to be very obedient and very reliable to perform their given tasks. A major role of the GSD has been that of a guard dog, so the dogs also had to be very protective of their owners. These characteristics translate into a dog who is very intelligent, highly trainable and extremely loyal. The German Shepherd Dog watches over the entire family and seems to be able to sense if someone is in

trouble or needs help. Likewise, the GSD is a wonderful protector of children and property.

Due to these protective instincts, the German Shepherd Dog is naturally wary of strangers. This is not to say that he is not a friendly dog, but he chooses whom to befriend based on his owner's attitude. "Any friend of yours is a friend of mine," the GSD seems to say to his owner, and he fiercely trusts his owner's judgment. The dog will warm up to people with whom he becomes familiar; he looks to his owner for clues about who is OK and who is not. Proper socialization and introduction to people from an early age are necessary to help the German Shepherd Dog become more accepting of the people he meets.

The GSD is noble and proud; he has a lot going for him and he knows it! A wonderful combination of stamina, athleticism, intelligence, grace and beauty, he personifies the virtues of "man's best friend."

OWNER SUITABILITY

Because the German Shepherd Dog is so devoted to his owner, it is only natural that he should thrive with an owner who can show him equal devotion. The GSD basks in his owner's attention. It is not necessarily true that the only type of person suitable to own a German Shepherd Dog is one who is home all day, but the owner who spends the day at work must plan to spend time with his or her GSD after work.

Meet other GSD owners just like you. On our GSD forums, you can chat about your German Shepherd Dog and ask other owners for advice on training, health issues and anything else about your favorite dog breed. Log onto **DogChannel.com/Club-GSD** for details!

Regular exercise is also important for the German Shepherd Dog. Remember, these dogs were bred to work and to be active. The breeders' original focus was on function. Because the pet GSD is not being used for his intended purpose, he must be active in other ways.

A GSD who lives at home with his owner cannot exercise himself; it is something that dog and owner need to participate in. It is not fair to the German Shepherd, who has patiently waited all day for his owner to return from work, for the owner to come home and promptly park himself on the couch for the remainder of the evening. Exercise is essential for the GSD's well-being — physically and mentally. It provides this athletic breed with much-needed activity; plus, it helps him feel like he has a purpose.

A house with a securely fenced yard is ideal for a smart German Shepherd Dog owner, as his GSD will have some freedom to run and play by himself. The dog should still be under the owner's supervision when off leash, but at least the dog will not be totally dependent on his owner for exercise. This does not make up for time spent with his favorite person — you — but it will at least give the dog some physical benefits. An owner who keeps a GSD in a house without a yard or in an apartment must make the commitment to regularly run, walk and play with his GSD.

The German Shepherd will fit into just about any family structure — adults, children, single people — as long as his owner takes into account his needs.

VERSATILITY AND AGILITY

Although your German Shepherd Dog may never be required to do more than provide companionship and protection to you and your family, you should be proud to consider the many other functions the breed can be called upon to perform.

The instinct to serve, which is innate to a GSD, is the foundation of his functional versatility along with his physical and mental traits of strength, size, endurance and intelligence. It would be fair to say that the majority of all service dogs in the world are German Shepherd Dogs. The potential for specific service duties lies within each shepherd, but in almost every case, professional training is required to harness such potential.

The German Shepherd Dog is also an excellent herding dog. This was his original function and remains a central factor in his modern versatility. His endurance, his rough coat, sure-footed speed, responsiveness and deeply rooted instinct to protect anything small or weak make him an ideal herding choice.

It is only in Germany that the German Shepherd Dog is a first choice among farmers and stock owners. In the United States and Great Britain, other native breeds that are more traditional and therefore more attractive — such as the Australian Shepherd and the Border Collie — are predominantly seen in herding capacities.

German Shepherd Dogs are known to be tough and protective, but they still need T-L-C from their loving owner.

German Shepherd Dogs were especially impressive as scout dogs for the military, often able to detect the presence of an enemy at 100 yards away. Countless human lives were saved by these dogs, but many of the animals were sacrificed during duty such as mine detecting.

Stemming from their role in the military, German Shepherd Dogs became the go-to dogs for police K9 units. In the pursuit and apprehension of criminals, GSDs have proven themselves valuable and rather more effective — certainly more humane — than guns. The dog's cool nerves and intelligence make him an excellent choice for crowd control. His scenting ability makes him invaluable in search-and-rescue work, as well as bomb and drug detection.

The skills and abilities of these functions are combined in schutzhund, a training and competition program that emphasizes the elements of protection. Schutzhund means "protection dog" in German. Schutzhund trials have existed since the early 1900s. They include tests for temperament, tracking and protection. Dogs are scored according to their performance in these areas and must exhibit complete obedience (despite distraction), confidence, courage, scenting ability, determination and concentration in tracking.

The preceding jobs and activities have stressed obedience founded upon the German Shepherd breed's natural proclivities. The GSD is not a particularly aggressive dog. He is, however, very protective of his family and property. This is the basis of the alertness and protective instinct that have made him a staple on security forces and an effective watchdog for the home and family.

The most noble and pride-stirring use of the German Shepherd Dog has been in the service of people with physical handicaps.

The GSD was the first dog used as a guide dog for the blind and later for deaf individuals. The dog's initial employment as guides for blind World War I veterans led to the conception of The Seeing Eye® foundation in 1929. Today this breed's traits of composure, intelligence and responsibility, combined with all of his other excellent attributes, continue to make him the first choice in this role to serve humankind.

WHAT MAKES A GERMAN SHEPHERD DOG?

The founder of the German Shepherd Dog breed, Capt. Max Emil Friedrich von Stephanitz, had some very specific ideas about what a GSD should be. Von Stephanitz wrote: "The most striking features of the correctly bred German Shepherd Dog are firmness of nerves, attentiveness, unshockability, tractability, watchfulness, reliability and incorruptibility together with courage, fighting tenacity and hardness." None of these qualities have anything to do with looks, structure, coat type or even herding ability. Instead, the hallmark quality of the German Shepherd Dog is that steady, somewhat aloof, alert and ultimately reliable temperament.

But anyone expecting a big waggy retriever-style dog, a cuddly lap dog, a

German Shepherd Dogs possess unlimited potential for adapting to different situations — particularly for service to their masters and their families. They are ultimately faithful and highly observant, and readily accept responsibility for many functions in the home and family. — William F. Gish, vice president of the German Shepherd Dog Club of Northern Virginia

couch-potato dog or a dog who is easy to outsmart, won't be happy with a German Shepherd. To know the GSD is not only to love him but to have the ability to train him successfully. "The things von Stephanitz said are very, very true," says Lori Nickerson, a GSD breeder in Bend, Ore., who participates in obedience, herding, tracking and agility with her dogs, and is chairman of the performance award of merit committee for the German Shepherd Dog Club of America. "But this breed isn't for everybody. This dog has to be part of the family in order to fulfill his potential. They are a one-family dog to a great extent, and they don't solicit attention from strangers. But you won't find a more trainable, courageous or loyal breed."

The German Shepherd is a tending dog. They are more inclined to keep the flock in one spot, acting as a living fence. For example, while a Border Collie moves a flock but waits at rest while the flock is grazing, a GSD remains vigilant and mobile, always aware of what's going on. He acts as a moving barrier to keep the flock safe.

That means you, and especially your children, are in many ways your German Shepherd Dog's flock. "They do try to keep

it's a Fact While sable is the most popular GSD color in the United States, it is decidedly less common in Germany. The most popular color in Germany is black and tan; however, both sable and black-and-tan coats tend to have richer, darker colors in Germany.

kids all together when they are playing, and even when you walk them, they will tend to go a little ahead, but keep checking back with you and circling you to make sure your perimeter is secure," Nickerson says.

This herding instinct also translates into lots and lots of energy because the German Shepherd must have the stamina to keep the flock contained all day long. "If you want a couch-potato dog, you do not want a German Shepherd," says Toni Liedtke, who works with GSDs in the Linn County (Iowa) Police Department. "If you've been at work all day, when you get home, your dog is going to want to go run five miles or go swimming or tracking or something. It's like the dog is thinking, 'Look, I've been good all day, and I haven't eaten your house. So we're going to go do something.' This is a breed that has to go and do. They are intense. You have to stimulate them physically and mentally, or they'll channel all that energy in some way you aren't going to like."

PHYSICAL CHARACTERISTICS

German Shepherd puppies have floppy ears that stand erect by 6 or 7 months of age. Some dogs have ears that never stand. Although taping most often can correct this fault, these dogs should be considered poor breeding choices.

Traditional depictions of the breed emphasize the black-and-tan coat with saddleback markings, but the German Shepherd Dog comes in a variety of colors such as black and red, black and cream, all black, all white, sable (with various colorations), black and silver, liver and blue. Breeders do not favor the white, liver or blue varieties; the American Kennel Club lists white dogs among the disqualifications for conformation (aka dog shows).

GSDs have double coats, with the coarser outer coat serving to resist water and debris, and the soft dense undercoat working to retain body heat during cold seasons. The coat can range from short and coarse to long and soft. Long-coated dogs, however, are not eligible for showing in the breed ring.

German Shepherd Dogs will shed all year long, with heavy shedding during the spring and fall. Grooming, however, is not difficult. Regular light brushing is all that is required. A hypoallergenic shampoo should be used during baths.

The main concern of every admirer of the German Shepherd Dog, however, is character. The animal should be courageous, intelligent, playful and safe with children, and obedient and responsive to his owner. These elements of sound disposition and utility supersede any and all physical ideals.

NOTABLE & QUOTABLE

Someone who isn't able to become a leader and take control of a situation should not own a German Shepherd Dog. Most of these dogs are pretty strong-willed. You can't let yourself be intimidated by these dogs. You need to give guidance, the right environment and training. You need to have fortitude and commitment to own one of these dogs.

— Linda Kury, rescue coordinator for the German Shepherd Dog Club of America

A German Shepherd wants a job, be it a family companion, sports star, police dog or therapy volunteer.

The Gentle German Shepherd

Jasmine had to testify in court, but Toni Liedtke knew it wouldn't be easy to get the scared 6-year-old to talk. As Victim Witness Coordinator for the Linn County Police Department in Cedar Rapids, Iowa, Liedtke often dealt with children, but this little girl, the victim of a crime, had no interest in sharing her story with adults, whom she had learned not to trust. Instead, she stared at a bulletin board covered with police dog cards in Liedtke's office. Suddenly, she turned to Liedtke and said, "Why isn't Charger on this board?"

Charger, one of the newest canine officers, hadn't had his card made yet, Liedtke explained. "But how do you know Charger?" she asked. Jasmine explained that her school had raised money for the police department, and in thanks, was allowed the opportunity to name the newest canine officer. "I named him," she said proudly. Suddenly, Liedtke had an idea.

She took the little girl on a tour of the courthouse, and introduced her to Charger's handler, Officer Graham Campshure. Jasmine got to pet Charger and play fetch with him. "You could see the change on her face whenever she was with that dog," Liedtke says. Finally, Jasmine said, "I'm not talking about this without Charger."

The little girl met with Charger on all her subsequent meetings with Liedtke, and while the judge wouldn't allow Charger in the courtroom while Jasmine had to testify, the faithful shepherd waited just outside the door. While testifying, Jasmine clutched three photographs of herself with Charger, and whenever she got scared and needed a break, she was allowed to go outside the courtroom and pet the ever-loyal GSD.

"I sincerely believe she never would have been able to go through all this and testify in court if it hadn't been for Charger," Liedtke says. "This dog helped her regain trust. The most amazing part was to see this tough, working police German Shepherd lying down on the floor with this little girl hugging and kissing and petting him, and then to know that 10 minutes later, he was out on the street apprehending criminals. But that's the German Shepherd."

A smart GSD owner will provide opportunities for his herding dog to fulfill his instinct to herd.

THE GERMAN SHEPHERD IN GENERAL

These serious, loving dogs make great additions to any family

COUNTRY OF ORIGIN: Germany

WHAT HIS FRIENDS CALL HIM: Alstian, Deutscher Schaferhund, Hasselhoff

SIZE: 22 to 26 inches, 60 to 90 pounds

COAT & COLOR: GSDs come in black and tan, black and red, solid black and sables of various shades. They have a double coat of medium length that consists of a dense outer coat and a downy undercoat. Long-coated varieties (pictured) aren't uncommon, but they are seen as a disqualification in the show ring (but not in homes of owners who enjoy the extra fluff!)

PERSONALITY TRAITS: These dogs are self confident and have an even temperament.

WITH KIDS: enjoys children

WITH OTHER PETS: does not play well with pets. He wants to herd them!

ENERGY LEVEL: middle to high

EXERCISE NEEDS: Daily outdoor exercise is a must for this breed.

GROOMING NEEDS: Smart owners brush their German Shepherd Dogs daily because this breed sheds heavily. Also, nails should be clipped regularly. Baths and ear cleaning should occur as needed.

TRAINING NEEDS: German Shepherd Dogs are intelligent and easy to train, especially when training begins at an early age. They perform well in obedience and other canine sports.

LIVING ENVIRONMENT: They are best suited to homes with large, fenced yards.

LIFESPAN: 10 to 12 years

HISTORY

It's no accident that the German Shepherd Dog is currently one of the most popular of the breeds recognized by the American Kennel Club. In the 90 years that the AKC has been registering dogs, the German Shepherd has been in the AKC Top 10 since 1948. This is due in part to the popularity of the 1950s television show, *Rin Tin Tin*, and partly to the high visibility the breed commands in military, police and assistance dog work.

However, popularity is a mixed blessing, as any conscientious German Shepherd breeder will tell you. It leads to indiscriminate breeding, overproduction and perpetuation of genetic flaws, such as poor temperaments and conformation faults. In years past, the German Shepherd Dog breed has suffered from more than its share of hip dysplasia, weak hocks (the equivalent of the ankle in humans) and unsound temperaments.

Not surprisingly, GSD *aficionados* are determined to improve the breed they love. Through culling, outcrossing, importing and a little soul-searching, they are pulling the German Shepherd Dog back from the abyss of irresponsible breeding.

Did You Know? **The German Shepherd Dog Club of America was established in 1913,** by B. H. Throop of Pennsylvania and Anne Tracy of New Jersey. By 1916, the club was incorporated and sponsored its first specialty show with 40 GSDs.

A breed based in temperament, the German Shepherd Dog is at home in the field.

IN THE BEGINNING

The particular qualifications that set the German Shepherd Dog apart from other breeds are numerous and evident from the first moment in the history of the breed. Considerations of companionship and domination aside, the first domesticated canines were utilized for practical and essential purposes such as guarding and controlling livestock. From the earlier herding dogs who helped shepherds with their flocks evolved light-gaited, weather-impervious, dependable canines, commonly categorized as sheepdogs.

In 1891, a group of German admirers of this rugged, unrefined dog formed the Phylax Society, named after the Greek word *phylaxis*, which means "to watch over or guard." The purpose of this organization was to standardize the varied collection of sheep-herding dogs into a breed of native German descent with a fixed appearance and character.

The Phylax Society lasted only three years, but its purpose and vision were continued by Capt. Max Emil Friedrich von Stephanitz, a man considered by many to be the single greatest force in the establishment of the German Shepherd Dog as a pure breed.

The originator of the breed was discovered by von Stephanitz on April 3, 1899, when he and another sheepdog enthusiast were attending an exhibition of these herding dogs. The dog they encountered was agile, powerful, alert and strongly adapted to his utilitarian purpose. To von Stephanitz, this particular animal seemed to be the perfect embodiment of the worker and guardian ideal that he held for this type of dog. The overt intelligence and desire to serve were apparent in the dog's temperament and belied his wild, wolfish appearance. Von Stephanitz bought the dog on the spot. His

From the moment they were created, German Shepherd Dogs were highly regarded as reliable, dedicated sheep-dogs, vigilantly watching over the flock.

original name, Hektor von Linksrhein, was changed to Horand von Grafrath, and he was registered as German Shepherd Dog, S.Z. 1, the first entry in von Stephanitz's new organization, Verein für Deutsche Schäferhunde. This was the beginning of the national German dog club known as the S.V., the largest individual breed club in the world.

Although most people consider von Stephanitz to be the father of the German Shepherd breed, the core dog he sought to start the breed already existed in Germany at the time. Creating the German Shepherd Dog was really just a matter of tweaking.

Because herding dogs at the time were bred for working ability, they varied drastically in appearance. Von Stephanitz applied the rigorous organization and his famous perfectionism to his breeding program to standardize appearance in a way that would maximize superior working ability.

Von Stephanitz eliminated hanging ears, wire coats and brindle dogs through refining a written standard and breeding for working ability as well as for conformation. However, he continually warned that the ability to work must come first and foremost.

HERDER PLUS

Some herding dogs nip at heels, some bark and some drive cattle ahead. Every herder has a particular method, but the German Shepherd Dog has always been an overachiever. "The breed's original function was to be the ultimate herding dog," says breeder Janice Buchanan of Harrisville, Utah. "Some breeds specialize in moving and cutting one or more sheep out of the flock, protecting the flock or keeping the flock together. The German Shepherd is designed to do all these and to do them without human direction."

That means German Shepherds use different methods than some other herding breeds like Welsh Corgis or Border Collies. This multitasking ability to herd and guard at the same time required a dog with a sound physique, superior intelligence and the ability to think for himself, even make decisions, qualities necessary in a herding dog who tends.

Often the victims of bandits and rivals, the people working as shepherds lived a dangerous existence and needed protection, too. German Shepherd Dogs worked without command and seemed to have an innate ability to know what to do and when, according to Susan Sullivan of Canterbury, Conn., who is an AKC Herding Group judge. "I like to think our dogs still have this uncanny intelligence that enables them to differentiate so well between friend and foe," she says.

Other qualities also helped the German Shepherd Dog excel as a herder. The dark and strong pigment made them stand out from the flock at a distance. In addition, the high efficiency of the German Shepherd Dog's nose and hearing helped alert the dog to danger or strays; an exceptional intelligence enabled the dog to analyze the surroundings and take the right course of action to protect the flock, without a human present

Max von Stephanitz didn't really invent or create the German Shepherd Dog. He preserved the breed by taking the best shepherds' dogs and breeding them selectively for more than just their abilities on stock. — breeder and American Kennel Club Herding Group judge Susan Sullivan of Canterbury, Conn.

to direct him; and a strong courage and resilience enabled him to face intruders or predators and defend his master's flock to the death, if necessary.

GSD DIVERSIFIES

With the advent of the Industrial Revolution during the late 18th and early 19th centuries, Europe changed dramatically. Cities grew and the need for working sheepdogs in Germany declined. Always a thinking man, von Stephanitz decided that the German Shepherd Dog's great versatility and many skills could be employed in other ways. He promoted his sheep-herding dogs as military and police dogs. The military scoffed at first, but von Stephanitz placed some with the police to prove themselves; they did so well that the military tried a few. By World War I, German Shepherd Dogs had become the military dogs of choice.

To accomplish his goal, von Stephanitz developed training procedures and tests in more formalized obedience work, tracking and protection, using the German Shepherd's natural skills in following directions, following a scent trail and protecting his flock and home. These programs formed the

The German Shepherd's ears, nose and eyes were perfected to aid in herding livestock.

The Most Famous German Shepherd

Rin Tin Tin conjures images of a handsome, heroic German Shepherd Dog from the silver screen and television, but few people know that the actual Rin Tin Tin almost didn't make it to Hollywood because he started out his life as a victim of war.

On Sept. 15, 1918, a war dog kennel in Lorraine, France, was bombed and destroyed, and would have been left for rubble if Corp. Lee Duncan hadn't insisted that his battalion inspect the kennel before moving on. All of the kennel's inhabitants had been killed except for one German Shepherd Dog, later named Betty, and her five pups. Duncan took two of the pups, a male and female, and the mother and other siblings went back to base camp. Duncan named the pups Rin Tin Tin and Nanette after the puppets that the French children gave to the American soldiers for good luck.

When World War I ended, Duncan arranged to have the puppies shipped to his home in Los Angeles, Calif. Unfortunately, Nanette died before Duncan could arrive to claim her. Rin Tin Tin survived, however, and Duncan continued to train him.

In 1922, Rin Tin Tin astounded audiences at a dog show by jumping 11½ feet, and Duncan was approached with the suggestion of putting Rin Tin Tin on camera. Duncan then began querying Hollywood movie studios about film concepts, but they all turned him down.

As fate would have it, Duncan and Rin Tin Tin ran into a movie crew filming a scene with an uncooperative wolf. Duncan insisted that Rin Tin Tin could do the scene in one take; they told him to get lost. He persisted, though, and they finally let the dog try the scene — success! Rin Tin Tin was signed to continue on in the film, *The Man From Hell's River*, and went on to make 26 movies for Warner Brothers, a studio that was on the brink of bankruptcy before the dog came along. They nicknamed Rin Tin Tin "the mortgage lifter."

America loved Rin Tin Tin, and he loved his life as a star, receiving 10,000 fan letters a week, and even a star on the Hollywood Walk of Fame (at 1623 Vine St.). Unfortunately, he died in the arms of actress Jean Harlow on Duncan's lawn just three days before he was to start his 27th movie. He was first buried at Duncan's home on Clubview Drive in Beverly Hills but was later moved to Cimetiëre des Chiens, a famous pet cemetery in Asnieres, a suburb just outside Paris.

The first German Shepherd Dog to come to America was imported by Otto Gross in 1905. Bred by P. Stretter, Mira of Dalmore was exhibited in the Miscellaneous Class and won ribbons. Mira's impact on the breed is merely anecdotal, and she was neither registered nor bred. Queen of Switzerland, owned by Adolph Vogt, was the first registered German Shepherd Dog in the American Kennel Club.

A herder at heart, the German Shepherd needs a home with room to roam and people to, um, herd.

basis for what has now become schutzhund, the rigorous sport testing the ability of a dog to track, perform obedience moves and protect on cue. Schutzhund is still an important part of German Shepherd Dog regulation in Germany today.

By the time World War I swept across Europe, the German Shepherd Dog became an invaluable part of the German army, delivering messages, guarding, tracking and helping the Red Cross. Soldiers from other countries observed the German Shepherd in action, and word of this incredibly intelligent and versatile service dog began to spread all over the world. The United States took notice.

Anti-German sentiment inspired temporary name changes to Shepherd Dog, Wolf Dog and Alsatian, but they didn't last. After the war, *Rin Tin Tin* hit televisions and the German Shepherd's popularity soared. As with any popular breed, many unscrupulous breeders compromised the quality of the breed in America, so that while some lines remained rigorously controlled, others developed health and temperament problems. The challenges of popularity still plague the German Shepherd Dog in America today.

In Germany, however, the German Shepherd Dog has long remained a breed fiercely protected by the S.V. Anyone planning to breed a German Shepherd Dog must first prove, through a series of rigorous tests, that the dog is worthy enough to justify producing offspring.

You have an unbreakable bond with your dog, but do you always understand him? Go online and download "Dog Speak," which outlines how dogs communicate. Find out what your German Shepherd Dog is saying when he barks, howls or growls. Go to **DogChannel.com/Club-GSD** and click on "Downloads."

IN AMERICA

During World War II, the American Kennel Club partnered with the newly formed Dogs for Defense organization, to recruit dogs to help with the war effort. People could send their own dogs to serve in the military. At first, the program accepted 30 different breeds, but soon limited the breeds to German Shepherd Dogs, Belgian Sheep Dogs, Doberman Pinschers, Farm Collies and Giant Schnauzers.

Between 1942 and 1945, more than 19,000 dogs enrolled in the program. About half didn't qualify as having adequate skills. Yet, even with these great numbers, the need for military dogs soon far exceeded the number of dogs available. Civilian trainers volunteered to train the dogs, and these "war dogs," as they were called, received specific training as sentries, scout or patrol dogs, and messenger or mine-detection dogs.

That working heritage hasn't kept GSDs out of the show ring. In 1907, the first German Shepherd Dog appeared in a dog show in the United States. Throughout the 1940s and 1950s, many American breeders imported German Shepherds from Germany to establish their kennel lines and participate in conformation shows.

At the time, German Shepherd Dogs from Germany set the standard for perfection. German-bred dogs and American-bred dogs certainly have diverged, as have working and show dogs in the United States. There has been a split, those who love the working sport and those who show their dogs. Even so, no matter what the country or what the work, the German Shepherd Dog remains among the most versatile of breeds.

MODERN-DAY GSD

The German Shepherd Dog we know today may not look or act exactly the same as that very first dog who inspired von Stephanitz to create the breed, but the original motivation — utility and intelligence — still prevails. They are family pets; conformation, obedience and herding champions; protection and guard dogs; and blind, hearing and impaired companions.

The German Shepherd Dog's function may have evolved over the years, but the basis for this breed has deep and solid roots. History has proven the ability of the German Shepherd to fill in where needed, to be available when asked and to accept the role given, no matter what. Because of that, it remains one of the most popular breeds in the world. Popularity follows function, and this is never more so than with the GSD.

The German Shepherd Dog, created more than 100 years ago, is basically the same today. GSD breeders strive to preserve the founder's perceptions and dreams. The dog is still intelligent, trainable, incredibly loyal and willing to die for his family. The German Shepherd Dog's history has called for a high standard, and that standard has given us the dog we have today.

NOTABLE & QUOTABLE *The size defined in the standard is meant to produce a dog who is agile, strong and substantial while being economical to feed, and the double coat enables the German Shepherd Dog to withstand a wider range of temperatures than most breeds.*
— *GSD breeder Janice Buchanan of Harrisville, Utah*

The GSD loves to work, but he also loves to play. Combine both of his loves by enrolling in a dog sport.

A SHEPHERD

As rough and tumble as the GSD can be, nothing is cuter than a German Shepherd puppy. His sweet face and round little body inspire *oohs* and *ahhs* from all who see them. That wonderful endearing quality, however, can also distract you from taking the time and doing the legwork necessary to find a puppy who's not only adorable, but also healthy in body and temperament as well. The key to finding the best German Shepherd puppy for you is to resist being charmed into a hasty decision and wait to find a responsible breeder. Then, you can have fun picking just the right puppy from a litter of those lovable faces.

You're going to have your GSD for 10 to 12 years, so the time you spend early on to locate a healthy, well-adjusted puppy from a reputable breeder will definitely pay off in the long run. Look for a dedicated and ethi-

> **In 1967, the German Shepherd Dog Club of America decided to disqualify white-coated dogs.** The German breed standard — the one most countries in the world recognize — also disqualifies white-coated dogs. After much work to establish the White Shepherd as a separate breed on the part of breeders and fanciers, the White Shepherd achieved United Kennel Club recognition as a separate breed from the German Shepherd Dog in May 1999.

it's a **Fact**

cal breeder who values good health and stable personalities, and who really cares what happens to the dog for the rest of his life.

Why is this so important? This is a breed with a unique personality who needs to be bred correctly by someone with experience who really knows what he or she is doing. If not, you may wind up with a dog who's overly aggressive, has a ton of health problems and doesn't even look like a German Shepherd Dog.

Be sure to avoid puppy mills and backyard breeders. Puppy mills are large-scale breeding operations that produce puppies in an assembly-line fashion without regard to health and socialization. Backyard breeders are typically well-meaning, regular pet owners who simply do not possess enough knowledge about the breed and breeding to produce healthy puppies.

The American Kennel Club (www.akc.org) and the United Kennel Club (www.ukcdogs. com) provide a list of breeders in good standing with their organizations. Visit their websites for more information.

EVALUATING BREEDERS

Once you have the names and numbers of breeders in your area, start contacting them to find out more about their breeding programs. But, before you contact them, prepare some questions to ask that will get you the information you need to know.

Prospective buyers interview breeders much the same way that a breeder should interview a buyer. Make a list of questions and record the answers so that you can compare them to the answers from other breeders whom you may interview later. The right questions are those that help you identify who has been in the breed a respectable number of years and who is actively showing their dogs. Ask in-depth questions regarding the genetic health of the parents, grandparents and great grandparents of any puppy you are considering. Ask what sort of genetic testing program the breeder adheres to.

You should look to see if a breeder actively shows his or her dogs in conformation events (aka dog shows). Showing indicates that the breeder is bringing out examples from his or her breeding program for the public to see. If there are any obvious problems, such as temperament or general conformation, they will be readily apparent. Also, the main reason to breed GSDs is to improve the quality of German Shepherd Dogs. If the breeder is not showing, then he or she is more likely to be breeding purely for the monetary aspect and may have less concern for the welfare and future of the breed.

Inquiring about health and determining the breeder's willingness to work with you in the future are also important for the potential puppy buyer to learn. The prospective buyer should see what kind of health guarantees the breeder gives. You should also find out if the breeder will be available for future consultation regarding your GSD, and find out if the breeder will take your dog back if something unforeseen happens.

Prospective buyers should ask plenty of questions, and in return, buyers should also

Did You Know?

Good Breeder Signs
When you visit a German Shepherd breeder, look around the home for:
- a clean, well-maintained facility
- no overwhelming odors
- overall impression of cleanliness
- socialized dogs and puppies

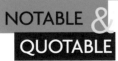

I ask buyers if they have ever owned a German Shepherd Dog. If so, I want to know what kind of relationship they had with their last dog. I insist on a fenced yard — electronic fencing is not good enough. I want to know who their veterinarian is. If they don't have one, I like to find out if they are receptive to my recommendations of vets in their area. — Donna Calabrese of Red Lion, Pa., a second-generation breeder and member of the German Shepherd Dog Club of America.

be prepared to answer questions posed by a responsible breeder who wants to make sure his or her puppy is going to a good home. Be prepared for a battery of questions from the breeder regarding your purpose for wanting this breed of dog and whether you can properly care for one. Avoid buying from a breeder who does little or no screening. If a breeder doesn't ask any questions, they are not concerned with where their pups end up. In this case, the dogs' best interests are probably not the breeder's motive for breeding.

The buyer should find a breeder who is willing to answer any questions they have and are knowledgeable about the history of the breed, health issues and about the background of their own dogs. Learn about a breeder's long-term commitment to the GSD breed and to his or her puppies after they leave the kennel.

Look for breeders who know their purpose for producing a particular litter, those who are knowledgeable in the pedigrees of their dogs and of the German Shepherd breed itself, and have had the necessary health screenings performed on the parents. They should also ask you for references to show that they are interested in establishing a relationship with you in con-

sideration for a puppy. If after one phone conversation with a breeder, the person is supplying you with an address in which to send a deposit, continue your search for a reputable breeder elsewhere.

CHOOSING THE RIGHT PUP

Once you have found a breeder you are comfortable with, your next step is to pick the right puppy. The good news is that if you have done your homework and found a responsible breeder, you can count on this person to give you plenty of help in choosing the right pup for your personality and lifestyle. In fact, most good breeders will recommend a specific puppy once they know what kind of dog you want.

After you have narrowed down the search and selected a reputable breeder, rely on the experience of the breeder to help you select your puppy. The selection of the puppy depends a lot on what purpose the pup is being purchased for. If the pup is being purchased as a show prospect, the breeder will offer his or her assessment of the pups that meet this criteria and be able to explain the strengths and faults of each pup.

Whether your GSD puppy is show- or pet-quality, a good, stable temperament is vital for a happy relationship. Generally, you want to avoid a timid puppy or a very dominant one. Temperament is very important, and a reputable breeder should spend a lot of time with the pups and be able to offer an evaluation of each pup's personality.

A reputable breeder might tell you which German Shepherd puppy is appropriate for your home situation and personality. They may not allow you to choose the puppy, although they certainly will take your preference into consideration.

Some breeders, on the other hand, believe it's important for you to be heavily involved in

Did You Know?

Healthy puppies have clear eyes, shiny coats, and are playful and friendly. An important factor in a puppy's long-term health and good temperament is the age he goes to his permanent home, which should be between 8 and 12 weeks. This gives the pups plenty of time to develop immunity and bond with their mom.

Questions to Expect
Be prepared for the breeder to ask you some questions, too.

children. This isn't a steadfast rule, and some breeders only insist on meeting the children to see how they handle puppies. It all depends on the breeder.

1. Have you previously owned a German Shepherd Dog?

The breeder is trying to gauge how familiar you are with the breed. If you have never owned one, illustrate your knowledge of GSDs by telling the breeder about your research.

2. Do you have children? What are their ages?

Some breeders are wary about selling a dog to families with younger

3. How long have you wanted a German Shepherd Dog?

This helps a breeder know if this purchase is an impulse buy or a carefully thought-out decision. Buying on impulse is one of the biggest mistakes owners can make. Be patient.

Join Club GSD to get a complete list of questions a breeder should ask you. Click on "Downloads" at:
DogChannel.com/Club-GSD

selecting a puppy from the litter. They will let their puppy buyers make the decision on which pup to take home because not everyone is looking for the same things in a dog. Some people want a quiet, laidback attitude. Others want an outgoing, active dog. When pups are old enough to go to their new homes at roughly 8 to 10 weeks of age, these breeders prefer you make your own decision because no one can tell at this age which pup will make the most intelligent or affectionate dog. The color, sex and markings are obvious,

German Shepherd puppies' ears are floppy, but they should stand erect by the time they are 6 or 7 months old.

With the popularity of German Shepherd Dogs, shelters and rescue groups across the country are often inundated with sweet, loving examples of the breed — from the tiniest puppies to senior dogs,

petite females to strapping males. Often, to get the German Shepherd Dog of your dreams, it takes a trip to the local shelter. Or, perhaps you could find your ideal dog waiting patiently in the arms of a foster parent at a nearby rescue group. It just takes a bit of effort, patience and a willingness to find the right dog for your family, not just the cutest dog on the block.

The perks of owning a GSD are plentiful: companionship, unconditional love, true loyalty and laughter, just to name a few. So why choose the adoption option? Because you literally will be saving a life!

Owners of adopted dogs swear they're more grateful and loving than any dog they've owned before. It's almost as if they knew what dire fate awaited them, and are so thankful to you. GSDs, known for their people-pleasing personalities, seem to embody this mentality wholeheartedly when they're rescued. And they want to give something back.

Another perk: Almost all adopted dogs come fully vetted, with proper medical treatment, vaccinations, medicine, as well as being spayed or neutered. Some are even licensed and microchipped.

Don't disregard older dogs, thinking the only good pair-up is between you and a puppy. Adult GSDs are more established behaviorally and personality-wise, helping to better mesh their characteristics with yours in this game of matchmaker. Puppies are always in high demand, so if you open your options to include adults, you will have a better chance of adopting quickly. Plus, adult dogs are often housetrained, more calm, chewproof, and don't need to be taken outside in the middle of the night ... five times ... in the pouring rain.

The American German Shepherd Rescue Association offers rescue support information (www.agsra. com) or log onto Petfinder.com (www.petfinder.com). The site's searchable database enables you to find a GSD in your area who needs a break in the form of a compassionate owner like you. More websites are listed in the Resources chapter on page 166.

but that is about all you can tell for sure at this age. Everything else being equal — size, health, etc. — some breeders suggest picking the pup whom you have a gut feeling for.

The chemistry between a buyer and puppy is important and should play a role in determining which pup goes to which home. When possible, make numerous visits to see the puppies, and in effect, let a puppy choose you. There usually will be one puppy who spends more time with a buyer and is more comfortable relaxing and sitting with or on a person.

CHECKING FOR GSD QUALITIES

Whether you are dealing with a breeder who wants to pick a pup for you or lets you make the decision alone, consider certain points when evaluating the pup who you may end up calling your own. The puppy should be friendly and outgoing, not skittish in any way. He should be forgiving of correction. He shouldn't be too terribly mouthy. The pup should readily follow you and be willing to snuggle in your lap and be turned onto his back easily without a problem.

Proper temperament is very important. A German Shepherd puppy who has a dominant personality requires an experienced owner who will be firm during training. A puppy who is a little shy requires heavy socialization to build his confidence.

You also can evaluate a GSD puppy's temperament on your own. The temperament of the pups can be evaluated by spending some time watching them. If you can visit the pups and observe them first together with their littermates, then you can see how they interact with each other. You may be able to pinpoint which ones are the bullies and which ones are more submissive. In general, look for a puppy who is more interested in you than in his littermates. Then, take each pup individually to a new location away from the rest of the litter. Put the puppy down on the ground, walk away and see how he reacts away from the security of his littermates. The puppy may be afraid at first, but he should gradually recover and start checking out the new surroundings.

Breeder Q&A

Here are some questions you should ask a breeder and the answers you want.

Q. How often do you have litters available?

A. You want to hear "once or twice a year" or "occasionally" because a breeder who doesn't have litters that often is probably more concerned with the quality of his puppies, rather than with making money.

Q. What kinds of health problems do GSDs have?

A. Beware of a breeder who says, "none." Every breed has health issues. For GSDs, some health problems include hip dysplasia, bloat, exocrine pancreatic insufficiency and degenerative myelopathy.

Get a complete list of questions to ask a GSD breeder — and the correct answers — at Club GSD. Log onto **DogChannel.com/Club-GSD** and click on "Downloads."

D-I-Y TEMPERAMENT TEST

Puppies come in a wide assortment of temperaments to suit almost everyone. If you are looking for a dog who is easily trainable and a good companion to your family, you most likely want a puppy with a medium temperament.

Temperament testing can help you determine the type of disposition your potential puppy possesses. A pup with a medium temperament will have the following reactions to these various tests, best conducted when the pup is 7 weeks old.

Step 1. To test a pup's social attraction and his confidence in approaching humans, coax him toward you by kneeling down and clapping your hands gently. A pup with a medium temperament comes readily, tail up or down.

Step 2. To test a pup's eagerness to follow, walk away from him while he is watching you. He should follow you readily, tail up.

Step 3. To see how a pup handles restraint, kneel down and roll the pup gently on his back. Using a light but firm touch, hold him in this position with one hand for 30 seconds. The German Shepherd pup should settle down after some initial struggle at first and offer some or steady eye contact.

Step 4. To evaluate a puppy's level of social dominance, stand up, then crouch down beside the pup and stroke him from head to back. A GSD puppy with a medium temperament — neither too dominant nor too submissive — should cuddle up to you and lick your face, or squirm and lick your hands.

Step 5. An additional test of a pup's dominance level is to bend over, cradle the pup under his belly with your fingers interlaced and palms up, and elevate him just off the ground. Hold him there for 30 seconds. The pup

Food intolerance is the inability of the dog to completely digest certain foods. Puppies who may have done very well on their mother's milk may not do well on cow's milk. The result of this food intolerance may be loose bowels, passing gas and stomach pains. These are the only obvious symptoms of food intolerance, which makes diagnosis difficult.

Regular visits to your breeder to check out his litter will ensure that you'll find the perfect GSD for you.

should not struggle and should be relaxed, or he should struggle and then settle down and lick you.

PHYSICAL FEATURES

To assess a puppy's health, take a deliberate, thorough look at each part of his body. Signs of a healthy puppy include bright eyes, a healthy coat, a good appetite and firm stool.

Watch for a telltale link between physical and mental health. A healthy German Shepherd Dog, as with any breed of puppy, will display a happier, more positive attitude than an unhealthy puppy. A German Shepherd puppy's belly should not be over extended or hard, as this may be a sign of worms. Also, if you are around the litter long enough to witness a bowel movement, the stool should be solid, and the pup should not show any signs of discomfort. Look into the pup's eyes, too; they should be bright and full of life.

When purchasing a German Shepherd puppy, buyers hear from breeders that these dogs are just like any other puppy — times 10! They are very smart, calculating, stubborn and often have their own agendas. If a prospective owner isn't willing to spend a fair amount of time with a GSD, then the breed is not for them. A German Shepherd Dog wants to be with people more than other dogs and is quite similar to a 7-year-old boy in the sense that he needs attention and consistent reinforcement for behavioral parameters. Once through adolescence, however, a GSD is the best friend, guardian and companion a person or family could have.

PUPPY PARTICULARS

Here are signs to look for when picking a puppy from a breeder. When in doubt, ask the breeder which puppy they think has the best personality/temperament to fit your lifestyle.

1. Look at the area where the pups spend most of their time. It's OK if they play outdoors part of the day, but they should sleep indoors at night so the pups can interact with people and become accustomed to hearing ordinary household noises. This builds a solid foundation for a well-socialized and secure German Shepherd puppy. The puppies' area should be clean, well-lit, have fresh drinking water and interesting toys.

2. Sure, you're only buying one puppy, but make sure to see all of the puppies in the litter. By 5 weeks of age, healthy pups will begin playing with one another and should be lively and energetic. It's OK if they're asleep when you visit, but stay long enough to see them wake up. Once they're up, they shouldn't be lethargic or weak, as this may be a sign of illness.

3. Pups should be confident and eager to greet you. A GSD pup who is shy or fearful and stays in the corner may be sick or insecure. Although some introverted pups come out of their shells later on, many do not. These dogs will always be fearful as adults and are not good choices for an active, noisy family with or without children, or for people who have never had a dog before. They frighten easily and will require a tremendous amount of training and socialization in order to live a happy life.

Choose a pup who is happy and eager to interact with you but reject the one who is either too shy or too bossy. These temperament types are a challenge to deal with, and require a tremendous amount of training to socialize. The perfect German Shepherd puppy personality is somewhere between the two extremes.

4. If it's feeding time during your visit, all pups should be eager to gobble up their food. A puppy who refuses to eat may signal illness.

5. The dog's skin should be smooth, clean and shiny without any sores or bumps. Puppies should not be biting or scratching at themselves continuously, which could signal fleas.

6. After 10 to 12 days, eyes should be open and clear without any redness or discharges. Pups should not be scratching at their eyes, as this may cause an infection or signal irritation.

7. Vomiting or coughing more than once is not normal. If so, a pup might be ill and should visit the veterinarian immediately.

8. Visit long enough to see the GSD pups eliminate. All stools should be firm without being watery or bloody. These are signs of illness or that a puppy has worms.

9. German Shepherd puppies should walk or run freely without limping.

10. A healthy GSD puppy who is getting enough to eat should not be skinny. You should be able to slightly feel his ribs if you rub his abdomen, but you should not be able to see the protruding ribs.

Healthy Puppy Signs

Here are a few things you should look for when selecting a puppy from a litter.

1. **NOSE:** It should be slightly moist to the touch, but there shouldn't be excessive discharge. The puppy should not be sneezing or sniffling persistently.

2. **SKIN AND COAT:** Your shepherd puppy's coat should be soft and shiny, without flakes or excessive shedding. Watch out for patches of missing hair, redness, bumps or sores. The pup should have a pleasant smell. Check for parasites, such as fleas or ticks.

3. **BEHAVIOR:** A healthy German Shepherd puppy may be sleepy, but he should not be lethargic. A healthy puppy will be playful at times, not isolated in a corner. You should see occasional bursts of energy and interaction with littermates. When it's mealtime, a healthy puppy will take an interest in his food.

There are more signs to look for when picking out the perfect German Shepherd puppy for your lifestyle. Download the list at **DogChannel.com/Club-GSD**

BREEDER PAPERS

Everything today comes with an instruction manual. When you purchase a GSD puppy, it's no different. A reputable breeder should give you a registration application; a sales contract; a health guarantee; your puppy's complete health records; a three-, four- or five-generation pedigree; and some general information on behavior, care, conformation, health and training.

Registration Application. This document from the AKC or UKC assigns your puppy a number and identifies the dog by listing his date of birth, the names of the parents and shows that he is registered as a purebred GSD. It doesn't prove whether or not your dog is a show- or a pet-quality GSD and doesn't provide any health guarantee.

Sales Contract. A reputable breeder should discuss the terms of the contract with you before asking you to sign it. This is a written understanding of both of your expectations and shows that the breeder cares about the pup's welfare throughout his life. The contract can include such terms as requiring you to keep the dog indoors at night, spaying or neutering if the puppy is not going to be a show dog, providing routine vet care and assurance that you'll feed your dog a healthy diet. Most responsible breeders will ask that you take your dog to obedience classes and earn a Canine Good Citizen title (an AKC training certification for dogs that exhibit good manners) before he is 2 years old. Many breeders also require new owners to have totally secure fencing and gates around their yard. German Shepherd Dogs are incredible escape artists, and they will find a way out of the yard if there's even the slightest opening.

Health Guarantee. This includes a letter from a veterinarian that the puppy has been examined and is healthy, and states that the breeder will replace your dog if he were to develop a genetic, life-threatening illness during his lifetime.

Health Records. Here's everything you want to know about your puppy's and his parents' health. It should include the dates the puppy was vaccinated, dewormed and examined by a veterinarian for signs of heart murmur, plus the parents' test results for the presence or absence of hip and elbow dysplasia, heart problems and luxated patellas.

Pedigree. Breeders should provide you with a copy of the puppy's three-, four- or five-generation pedigree. Many breeders also have photos of the dog's ancestors that they will proudly share with you.

Extra Information. The best breeders pride themselves on handing over a notebook full of the latest information on GSD behavior, care, conformation, health and training. Be sure to read it because it will provide valuable help while raising your German Shepherd Dog.

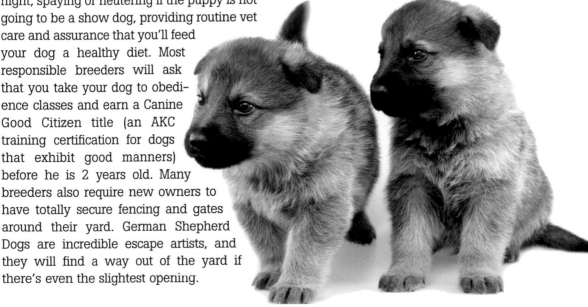

ESSENTIALS

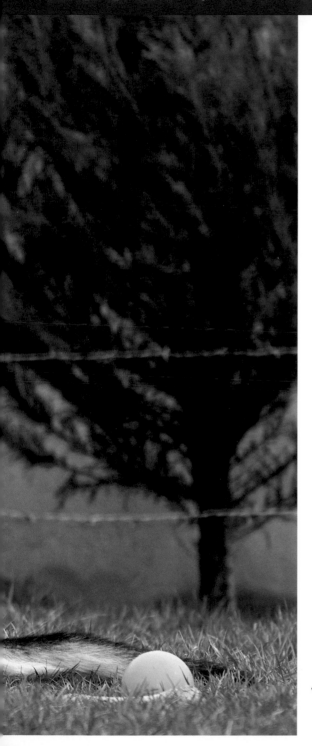

D on't for one second think that a GSD would prefer to live out in the open with shepherds! He, like every other breed, wants to live in the best accommodations with plenty of toys, soft bedding and other "luxuries." Your home is now his home, too; and, before you even bring that new puppy or rescue dog into his new forever home, be a smart owner and make your home accessible for him.

In fact, in order for him to grow into a stable, well-adjusted dog, he has to feel comfortable in his surroundings. Remember, he is leaving the warmth and security of his mother and littermates, as well as the familiarity of the only place he has ever known, so it is important to make his transition to your home — his new home — as easy as possible.

PUPPY-PROOFING

Aside from making sure that your GSD will be comfortable in your home, you also have to ensure that your home is safe, which means taking the proper precautions to keep your pup away from things that are dangerous for him.

it's a Fact

Dangers lurk indoors and outdoors. Keep your curious GSD from investigating your shed and garage. Antifreeze and fertilizers, such as those you would use for roses, can kill any dog. Keep these items on high shelves that are out of reach.

SMART TIP!

A well-stocked toy box should contain three main categories of toys.

1. **action** — anything that you can throw or roll and get things moving
2. **distraction** — durable toys that make dogs work for a treat
3. **comfort** — soft, stuffed "security blankets"

Puppy-proof your home inside and out before bringing your GSD home for the first time. Place breakables out of reach. If he is limited to certain places within the house, keep potentially dangerous items in off-limit areas. If your GSD is going to spend time in a crate, make sure that there isn't anything near it that he can reach if he sticks his curious little nose or paws through the openings.

A smart owner will provide plenty of engaging toys to distract his GSD from chewing on potentially harmful — or valuable — items.

The outside of your home must also be safe. Your pup will want to run and explore the yard, and he should be granted that freedom — as long as you are there to supervise. Do not let a fence give you a false sense of security; you would be surprised how crafty and persistent a German Shepherd puppy can be in figuring out how to dig under a fence or squeeze his way through holes. The remedy is to make the fence well-embedded into the ground. Be sure to repair or secure any gaps in the fence. Check the fence periodically to ensure that it is in good shape and make repairs as needed; a very determined puppy may work on the same spot until he is able to get through.

The following are a few common problem areas to watch out for in the home.

■ **Electrical cords and wiring:** No electrical cord or wiring is safe. Many office-supply stores sell products to keep wires gathered under computer desks, as well as products that prevent office chair wheels (and puppy teeth) from damaging electrical cords. If you have exposed cords and wires, these products aren't very expensive and can be used to keep a puppy out of trouble.

■ **Trash cans:** Don't waste your time trying to train your GSD not to get into the trash. Simply put the garbage behind a cabinet door and use a child-safe lock, if necessary. Dogs love bathroom trash, which consists of items that can be extremely dangerous (i.e., cotton balls, cotton swabs, used razors, dental floss, etc.)! Put the bathroom trash can in a cabinet under the sink and make sure you always shut the door to the bathroom.

■ **Household cleaners:** Make sure your German Shepherd puppy doesn't have access to any of these deadly chemicals. Keep them behind closed cabinet doors, using child-safe locks, if necessary.

A fenced yard is a must for the agile and active German Shepherd Dog.

■ **Pest control sprays and poisons:** Chemicals to control ants or other pests should never be used in the house, if possible. Your GSD pup doesn't have to directly ingest these poisons to become ill; if he steps in the poison, he can experience toxic effects by licking his paws. Roach motels and other toxic pest traps are also yummy to dogs, so don't drop these behind couches or cabinets; if there's room for a roach motel, there's room for a determined GSD.

■ **Fabric:** Here's one you might not think about: Some puppies have a habit of licking blankets, upholstery, rugs or carpets. Though this habit seems fairly innocuous, over time the fibers from the upholstery or carpet can accumulate in the dog's stomach and cause a blockage. If you see your dog licking these items, remove the item or prevent him from having contact with it.

■ **Prescriptions, painkillers, supplements and vitamins:** Keep all medications in a cabinet. Also, be very careful when taking your prescription medications, supplements or vitamins: How often have you dropped a pill? You can be sure that your GSD puppy will be in between your legs and will snarf up the pill before you even start to say "No!" Dispense your own pills carefully and without your German Shepherd present.

■ **Miscellaneous loose items:** If it's not bolted to the floor, your puppy is likely to give the item a taste test. Socks, coins, children's toys, game pieces, cat toys — you name it. If it's on the floor, it's worth a try. Make sure the floors in your home are picked up and free of clutter.

FAMILY INTRODUCTIONS

Everyone in the house will be excited about the puppy's homecoming and will want to pet and play with him, but it is best to make the introduction low-key so as not to overwhelm your puppy. He already will be apprehensive. It is the first time he has been separated from his mother, littermates and breeder, and the ride to your home is likely to be the first time he has been in a car. The last thing you want to do is smother your GSD pup, as this will only frighten him further. This is not to say that human contact is unnecessary at this stage because this is the time when a connection between the pup and his human family is formed. Gentle petting and soothing words should help console your GSD, as well as putting him down and letting him explore on his own (under your watchful eye, of course).

Your pup may approach the family members or may busy himself with exploring for a while. Gradually, each person should spend some time with the pup, one at a time, crouching down to get as close to the GSD's level as possible, letting him sniff their hands before petting him gently. He definitely needs human attention, and he needs to be touched; this is how to form an immediate bond. Just remember that the pup is experiencing a lot of things for the first time, all at once. There are new people, new noises, new smells and new things to investigate. Be gentle, be affectionate and be as comforting as you can possibly be.

NOTABLE & QUOTABLE

The first thing you should always do before your puppy comes home is to lie on the ground and look around. You want to be able to see everything your puppy is going to see. For the puppy, the world is one big chew toy.

— *Cathleen Stamm, rescue volunteer in San Diego, Calif.*

PUP'S FIRST NIGHT HOME

You have traveled home with your new puppy safely in his crate. He may have already been to the vet for a thorough check-up — he's been weighed, his papers examined, perhaps he's even been vaccinated and dewormed as well. Your GSD has met and licked the whole family, including the excited children and the less-than-happy cat. He's explored his area, his new bed, the yard and everywhere else he's permitted. He's eaten his first meal at home and relieved himself in the proper place. Your GSD has heard lots of new sounds, smelled new friends and seen more of the outside world than ever before. This was just the first day! He's worn out and is ready for bed — or so you think!

Remember, this is your puppy's first night to sleep alone. His mother and littermates

are no longer at paw's length, and he's scared, cold and lonely. Be reassuring to your new family member. This is not the time to spoil your GSD and give in to his inevitable whining.

Puppies whine. They whine to let others know where they are and hopefully to get company out of it. Place your GSD puppy in his new bed or crate in his room and close the door. Mercifully, he may fall asleep with-

SMART TIP!

When you are unable to watch your German Shepherd puppy, put her in a crate or an exercise pen on an easily cleanable floor. If she has an accident on carpeting, clean it completely and meticulously, so that it doesn't smell like her potty forever.

out a peep. If the inevitable occurs, ignore the whining; he is fine. Do not give in and visit your GSD puppy. He will fall asleep eventually.

Many breeders recommend placing a piece of bedding from his former home in his new bed so that he will recognize the scent of his littermates. Others still advise placing a hot water bottle in his bed for warmth. The latter may be a good idea provided the pup doesn't attempt to suckle.

Your GSD's first night can be somewhat terrifying for him. Remember that you set the tone of nighttime at your house. Unless you want to play with your pup every night at 10 p.m., midnight and 2 a.m., don't initiate the habit. Your family will thank you, and so will your pup!

PET-SUPPLY STORE SHOPPING

It's fun shopping for new things for a new puppy. From training to feeding and sleeping to playing, your new German Shepherd Dog will need a few items to make life comfy, easy and fun. Be prepared and visit your local pet-supply store before you bring home your new family member.

◆ **Collar and ID tag:** Accustom your dog to wearing a collar the first day you bring him home. Not only will a collar and ID tag help your puppy in the event that he becomes lost, but collars are also an important training tool. If your GSD gets into trouble, the collar will act as a handle, helping you divert him to a more appropriate behavior. Make sure the collar fits snugly enough so that your shepherd cannot wriggle out of it, but is loose enough so that it will not be uncomfortably tight around his neck. You should be able to fit a finger between your pup's neck and the collar. Collars come in many styles, but for starting out, a simple buckle collar with an easy-release snap works great.

SMART TIP!

9-1-1! If you don't know whether the plant, food or "stuff" your German Shepherd just ate is toxic to dogs, call the ASPCA's Animal Poison Control Center (888-426-4435). Be prepared to provide your puppy's age and weight, her symptoms — if any — and how much of the plant, chemical, or substance she ingested, as well as how long ago you think she came into contact with the substance. The ASPCA charges a consultation fee for this service.

◆ **Leash:** For training or just for taking a stroll down the street, a leash is your GSD's vehicle to explore the outside world. Like collars, leashes come in a variety of styles and materials. A 6-foot nylon leash is a popular choice because it is lightweight and durable. As your pup grows and gets used to walking on the leash, you may want to purchase a flexible leash. These leads allow you to extend the length to give your dog a broader area to explore or to shorten the length to keep your dog closer to you.

◆ **Bowls:** Your GSD will need two bowls: one for water and one for food. You may want two sets of bowls, one for inside and one for outside, depending on where your dog will be fed and where he will be spending time. Bowls should be sturdy enough so that they don't tip over easily. (Most have reinforced bottoms that prevent tipping.) Bowls usually are made of metal, ceramic or plastic, and should be easy to clean.

◆ **Crate:** A multipurpose crate serves as a bed, housetraining tool and travel carrier. It also is the ideal doggie den — a bedroom of sorts — that your GSD can retire to when

Food-stuffed chew toys are great for keeping your dog busy and entertained while you are doing other things.

Playing with toys from puppyhood encourages good behavior and social skills throughout your dog's life. A happy, playful dog is a content and well-adjusted one. Also, because all puppies chew to soothe their gums and help loosen puppy teeth, dogs should always have easy access to several different toys.
— dog trainer and author Harrison Forbes of Savannah, Tenn.

SMART TIP!

Keep a crate in your vehicle and take your GSD along when you visit the drive-thru at the bank or your favorite fast-food restaurant. She can watch interactions, hear interesting sounds and maybe earn a dog treat.

he wants to rest or just needs a break. The crate should be large enough for your dog to stand in, turn around and lie down. You don't want any more room than this — especially if you're planning on using the crate to housetrain your dog — because he will eliminate in one corner and lie down in another. Get a crate that is big enough for your dog when he is an adult. Then, use dividers to limit the space when he's a puppy.

◆ **Bed:** A plush doggie bed will make sleeping and resting more comfortable for your GSD. Dog beds come in all shapes, sizes and colors, but your dog just needs one that is soft and large enough for him to stretch out on. Because puppies and rescue dogs may not always be housetrained, it's helpful to buy a bed that can be easily washed. If your German Shepherd Dog will be sleeping in a crate, a nice crate pad and a small blanket that he can "burrow" in will help him feel more at home. Replace the blanket if it becomes ragged and starts to fall apart because your German Shepherd's nails could get caught in it.

◆ **Gate:** Similar to those used for toddlers, gates help keep your GSD confined to one room or area when you can't supervise him. Gates also work to keep your dog out of areas you don't want him in. Gates are

Dogs like to chew and eat just about anything. Always try to supervise your dog when you are outside.

available in many styles. Make sure you choose one with openings small enough so your puppy can't squeeze through the bars or any gaps.

◆ **Toys:** Keep your dog occupied and entertained by providing him with an array of fun toys. Teething puppies like to chew — in fact, chewing is a physical need for pups as they are teething — and everything from your shoes to the leather couch to the fancy rug are fair game. Divert your GSD's chewing

When out and about, make sure your GSD is wearing a durable collar and leash.

It may seem cool to let your GSD hang his head out the window, but it's just an accident waiting to happen. Always crate or securely fasten him inside the vehicle.

instincts with durable toys like bones made of nylon or hard rubber.

Other fun toys include rope toys, treat-dispensing toys and balls. Make sure the toys and bones don't have small parts that could break off and be swallowed, causing your dog to choke. Stuffed toys can become destuffed, and an overly excited puppy may ingest the stuffing or the squeaker. Check your GSD's toys regularly and replace them if they become frayed or show signs of wear.

◆ **Cleaning supplies:** Until your German Shepherd puppy is housetrained, you will be doing a lot of cleaning. Accidents will occur, which is acceptable in the beginning because the puppy doesn't know any better. All you can do is be prepared to clean up any accidents. Old rags, towels, newspapers and a stain-and-odor remover are good to have on hand.

Funny Bone

To err is human; to forgive, canine.

— *Anonymous*

BEYOND THE BASICS

The basic items discussed previously are the bare necessities. You will find out what else you and your new dog need as you go along — grooming supplies, flea/tick protection — and these things will vary depending on your situation. It is important, however, that you have everything you need to make your German Shepherd Dog comfortable in his new home.

Some ordinary household items make great toys for your GSD — as long you make sure they are safe. Tennis balls, plastic water bottles, old towels and more can be transformed into fun with a little creativity. You can find a list of homemade toys at **DogChannel.com/Club-GSD**

HOUSETRAINING

Unexciting as it may be, the housetraining part of puppy rearing greatly affects the budding relationship between a smart owner and his puppy — particularly when it becomes an area of ongoing contention. Fortunately, armed with suitable knowledge, patience and common sense, you'll find housetraining progresses at a relatively smooth rate. That leaves more time for the important things, like cuddling your adorable puppy, showing him off and laughing at his high jinks.

The answer to successful housetraining is total supervision and management — crates, tethers, exercise pens and leashes — until you know your dog has developed preferences for outside surfaces (grass, gravel, concrete) instead of carpet, tile or hardwood, and knows that potty happens outside.

IN THE BEGINNING

For the first two to three weeks of a puppy's life, his mother helps the pup to eliminate. The mother also keeps the whelping box or "nest area" clean. When pups begin to walk around and eat on their own, they choose where they eliminate. You can train your puppy to relieve himself wherever

it's a Fact **Ongoing housetraining difficulties may indicate your pup has a health problem,** warranting a vet check. A urinary infection, parasites, a virus, and other nasty issues greatly affect your puppy's ability to hold pee or poop.

you choose, but this must be somewhere suitable. You should bear in mind from the outset that when your puppy is old enough to go out in public places, you must be considerate and pick up after him. You will always have to carry with you a small plastic bag or poop scoop.

Outdoor training includes such surfaces as grass, soil and concrete. Indoor training usually means training your dog on newspaper. When deciding on the surface and location that you will want your GSD to use, be sure it is going to be permanent. Training your

dog on grass and then changing two months later is extremely difficult for dog and owner.

Next, choose the cue you will use each and every time you want your puppy to eliminate. "Let's go," "hurry up" and "potty" are examples of cues commonly used by smart dog owners.

Get in the habit of giving your puppy the chosen relief cue before you take him out. That way, when he becomes an adult, you will be able to determine if he wants to go out when you ask him. A confirmation will be signs of interest, such as wagging his tail, watching you intently or going to the door.

LET'S START WITH THE CRATE

Clean animals by nature, dogs dislike soiling where they sleep and eat. This fact makes a crate a useful tool for housetraining. When purchasing a new crate, consider that an appropriately sized crate will allow adequate room for an adult dog to stand

If you rescue an older German Shepherd, use the same housetraining combination that you would on a pup: consistency and patience.

full-height, lie on his side without scrunching and turn around easily. If debating plastic versus wire crates, short-haired breeds sometimes prefer the warmer, draft-blocking quality of plastic, while furry dogs often like the cooling airflow of a wire crate.

Some crates come with a movable wall that reduces the interior size to provide enough space for your puppy to stand, turn and lie down, while not allowing him room to soil one end and sleep in the other. The problem is that if your puppy goes potty in the crate anyway, the divider forces him to lie in his own excrement.

This can work against you by desensitizing your puppy against his normal, instinctive revulsion to resting where he has just eliminated. If scheduling permits you or a responsible family member to clean the crate soon after it's soiled, then you can continue to cratetrain because limiting crate size does encourage your puppy to hold it. Otherwise, give him enough room to move away from an unclean area until he's better able to control his elimination.

Needless to say, not every German Shepherd puppy adheres to this guideline. If your GSD moves along at a faster pace, thank your lucky stars. Should he progress slower, accept it and remind yourself that he'll improve. Be aware that puppies frequently hold it longer at night than during the day. Just because your puppy sleeps for six or more hours through the night, it does not mean he can hold it that long during the more active daytime hours.

One last bit of advice on the crate: Place it in the corner of a high-traffic room, such

as the family room or kitchen. Social and curious by nature, dogs like to feel included in family happenings. Creating a quiet retreat by putting the crate in an unused area may seem like a good idea, but results in your puppy feeling insecure and isolated. Watching his people pop in and out of the crate room reassures your puppy that he's not forgotten.

A PUP'S GOT NEEDS

Your puppy needs to relieve himself after play periods, after each meal, after he has been sleeping and any time he indicates that he is looking for a place to urinate or defecate.

The urinary and intestinal tract muscles of very young puppies are not fully developed. Therefore, like human babies, pup-

If your puppy has an accident indoors, don't scold him. Instead, take him to his proper potty area and give him a treat for finishing there.

pies need to relieve themselves frequently. Take your puppy out often — every hour for an 8-week-old, for example — and always immediately after sleeping and eating. The older the puppy, the less often he will need to relieve himself. Finally, as a mature, healthy adult, he will require only three to five relief trips per day.

HOUSING HELPS

Because the types of housing and control you provide for your GSD puppy have a direct relationship on the success of house-training, you must consider the various aspects of both before beginning training. Taking a new puppy home and turning him loose in your house can be compared to turning a child loose in a sports arena and telling the child that the place is all his! The sheer enormity of the place would be too much for him to handle. Instead, offer the puppy clearly defined areas where he can play, sleep, eat and live. A room of the house where the family gathers is the most obvious choice.

Puppies are social animals and need to feel like they are a part of the pack right from the start. Hearing your voice, watching you while you are doing things and smelling you nearby are all positive reinforcers that he is now a member of your pack. Usually a family room, the kitchen or a nearby adjoining

Reward your pup with a high-value treat immediately after he potties to reinforce going in the proper location, then play for a short time afterward. This teaches that good things happen after pottying outside! — Victoria Schade, certified pet dog trainer, from Annandale, Va.

If you acquire your puppy at 8 weeks of age, expect to take her out at least six to eight times a day. By the time she's about 6 months old, potty trips will be down to three or four times a day. A rule of thumb is to take your puppy out in hourly intervals equal to her age in months.

IN CONTROL

By control, we mean helping the puppy to create a lifestyle pattern that will be compatible to that of his human pack (you!). Just as we guide children to learn our way of life, we must show our GSD pup when it is time to play, eat, sleep, exercise and entertain himself.

Your puppy should always sleep in his crate. He should also learn that, during times of household confusion and excessive human activity, such as at breakfast when family members are preparing for the day, he can play by himself in relative safety and comfort in his designated area. Each time you leave your GSD alone, he should understand exactly where he is supposed to stay.

Puppies are chewers. They cannot tell the difference between lamp cords, television wires, shoes or table legs. Chewing into a television wire, for example, can be fatal to the puppy, while a shorted wire can start a fire in the house.

breakfast area is ideal for providing safety and security for puppy and owner.

Within that room, there should be a smaller area that your GSD puppy can call his own. An alcove, a wire or fiberglass dog crate, or a fenced (not boarded!) corner from which he can view the activities of his new family will be fine. The designated area should be lined with clean bedding and a toy. Water must always be available, in a nonspill container, once your dog is housetrained.

If the puppy chews on the arm of the chair when he is alone, you probably will discipline him angrily when you get home. Thus, he makes the association that your coming home means he is going to be punished. (He will not remember chewing the chair and is incapable of making the association of the discipline with his naughty deed.)

Other times of excitement, such as family parties, can be fun for your puppy, provided that he can view the activities from the security of his designated area. He is not underfoot, and he is not being fed all sorts of tidbits that will probably cause him stomach distress, yet he still feels a part of the fun.

SCHEDULE A SOLUTION

A puppy should be taken to his relief area each time he is released from his designated area, after meals, after play sessions and when he first awakens in the morning (at 8 weeks of age, this can mean 5 a.m.!). The

Did You Know? White vinegar is a good odor remover if you don't have any professional cleaners on hand; use one-quarter cup vinegar to one quart of water.

Keep potty trips to your puppy's relief area short. Stay no more than 5 or 6 minutes, and then return to inside the house. If your puppy potties during that time, lavishly praise him and then immediately take him indoors. If he does not potty, but he has an accident later when you go back indoors, pick him up, say "No! No!" and return to his relief area. Wait a few minutes, then return to the house again. Never hit your German Shepherd puppy or rub his face in urine or excrement when he has had an accident.

puppy will indicate that he's ready "to go" by circling or sniffing busily — do not misinterpret these signs. For a puppy less than 10 weeks of age, a routine of taking him out every hour is necessary. As your puppy grows, he will be able to wait for longer periods of time.

Clean accidents up thoroughly, so your puppy won't smell the area and think it's an approved potty spot.

10 HOUSETRAINING HOW-TOs

1. Decide where you want your German Shepherd Dog to eliminate. Take her there every time until she gets the idea. Pick a spot that's easy to access. Remember, puppies have very little time between "gotta go" and "oops."

2. Teach an elimination cue, such as "go potty" or "get busy." Say this every time you take your GSD to eliminate. Don't keep chanting the cue, just say it once or twice then keep quiet so you won't distract your dog.

3. Praise calmly when your dog eliminates, but stand there a little longer in case there's more.

4. Keep potty outings for potty only. Take the dog to the designated spot, tell her "go potty" and just stand there. If she needs to eliminate, she will do so within five minutes.

5. Don't punish for potty accidents; punishment can hinder progress. If you catch your GSD in the act indoors, verbally interrupt but don't scold. Gently carry or lead your pup to the approved spot, let her finish, then praise.

6. If it's too late to interrupt an accident, scoop the poop or blot up the urine afterward with a paper towel. Immediately take your dog and her deposit (gently!) to the potty area. Place the poop or trace of urine on the ground and praise the pup. If she sniffs at her waste, praise more. Let your GSD know you're pleased when her waste is in the proper area.

7. Keep track of when and where your GSD eliminates — that will help you anticipate potty times. Regular meals mean regular elimination, so feed your dog scheduled, measured meals instead of free-feeding (leaving food available at all times).

8. Hang a bell on a sturdy cord from the doorknob. Before you open the door to take your puppy out for potty, shake the string and ring the bell. Most dogs soon realize the connection between the bell ringing and the door opening, then they'll try it out for themselves.

9. Dogs naturally return to re-soil where they've previously eliminated, so thoroughly clean up all accidents. Household cleaners usually will do the job, but special enzyme solutions may work better.

10. If the ground is littered with too much waste, your GSD may seek a cleaner place to eliminate. Scoop the potty area daily, leaving behind just one "reminder."

Once indoors, put your GSD puppy in his crate until you have had time to clean up his accident. Then release him to the family area and watch him more closely than before. Chances are, his accident was a result of your not picking up his potty signals or waiting too long before offering him the opportunity to relieve himself. Never hold a grudge against your puppy for accidents.

Let your puppy learn that going outdoors means it is time to relieve himself, not to play. Once trained, he will be able to play indoors and outdoors and still differentiate between the times for play versus the times for relief.

Help him develop regular hours for naps, being alone, playing by himself and just resting — all in his crate. Encourage him to entertain himself while you are busy elsewhere. Let him learn that having you nearby is comforting, but it is not your main purpose in life to provide him with undivided attention.

Each time you put your German Shepherd puppy in his own area, use the same command, whatever suits you best. Soon he will run to his crate or special area when he hears you say those words.

Remember that one of the primary ingredients in housetraining your puppy is control. Regardless of your lifestyle, there will always be occasions when you will need to have a place where your dog can stay and be happy and safe. Cratetraining is the answer for now and in the future.

A few key elements are really all you need for a successful housetraining method: consistency, frequency, praise, control and supervision. By following these procedures with a normal, healthy puppy, you and your German Shepherd Dog will soon be past the stage of accidents and ready to move on to a full and rewarding life together.

So the first day doesn't go so great. Don't panic, and stay positive. Your GSD puppy will get the hang of it in time.

JOIN OUR ONLINE Club GSD®

Having housetraining problems with your GSD? Ask other German Shepherd owners for advice and tips. Log onto **DogChannel.com/Club-GSD** and click on "Community."

EVERYDAY CARE

Your selection of a veterinarian for your dog should be based on personal recommendations of the doctor's skills with dogs, and, if possible, especially German Shepherd Dogs. If the veterinarian is based nearby, it will be helpful and more convenient because you might have an emergency or need to make multiple visits for treatments.

FIRST STEP: SELECT THE RIGHT VET

All licensed veterinarians are capable of dealing with routine medical issues such as infections and injuries, as well as the promotion of good health (like vaccinations). If the problem affecting your GSD is more complex, your vet will refer you to someone with more detailed knowledge of what is wrong. This usually will be a specialist such as a veterinary dermatologist or veterinary ophthalmologist.

Veterinary procedures are very costly and, as treatments improve, they are going to become more expensive. It is quite acceptable to discuss matters of cost with your vet; if there is more than one treatment option, cost may be a factor in deciding which route to take.

Smart owners will look for a veterinarian before they actually need one. For newbie pet owners, start looking for a veterinarian a month or two before you bring home your new German Shepherd puppy. That will give you time to meet candidate veterinarians, check out the condition of the clinic, meet the staff and see who you feel most comfortable with. If you already have a GSD puppy, look sooner rather than later, preferably not in the midst of a veterinary health crisis.

Second, list the qualities that are important to you. Points to consider or investigate:

Convenience: Proximity to your home, extended hours or drop-off services are helpful for people who work regular business hours, have a busy schedule or don't want to drive far. If you have mobility issues, finding a vet who makes house calls or a service that provides pet transport might be particularly important.

Size: A one-person practice ensures that you will always be dealing with the same vet during each and every visit. "That person can really get to know you and your dog," says Bernadine Cruz, D.V.M., of Laguna Hills Animal Hospital in Laguna Hills, Calif. The downside, though, is that the sole practitioner does not have the immediate input of another vet, and if your vet becomes ill or takes time off, you are out of luck.

The multiple-doctor practice offers consistency if your GSD needs to come in unexpectedly on a day when your veterinarian isn't there. Additionally, your vet can quickly consult with his colleagues within the clinic if he's unsure about a diagnosis or a treatment.

If you find a veterinarian within that practice who you really like, you can make your appointments with that individual, establishing the same kind of bond that you would with the solo practitioner.

Appointment Policies: Some practices are by-appointment only, which could minimize your wait time. However, if a sudden problem arises with your GSD and the veterinarians are booked up, they might not be able to squeeze your pet in that day. Some clinics are drop-in only, which is great for impromptu or crisis visits, but without scheduling may involve longer waits to see the next available veterinarian. Some practices offer the best of both worlds by maintaining an appointment schedule but also keeping slots open throughout the day for walk-ins.

Basic vs. Full Service vs. State-of-the-Art: A veterinarian practice with high-tech equipment offers greater diagnostic capabilities and treatment options, important for tricky or difficult cases. However, the cost of pricey equipment is passed along to the client, so you could pay more for routine procedures — the bulk of most pets' appointments. Some practices offer boarding, grooming, training classes and other services on the premises — conveniences some pet owners appreciate.

Fees and Payment Polices: How much is a routine visit? If there is a significant price difference, ask why. If you intend to carry health insurance on your GSD or want to pay by credit card, check that the clinic accepts those payment options.

FIRST VET VISIT

It is much easier, less costly and more effective to practice preventive medicine than to fight bouts of illness and disease. Properly bred puppies of all breeds come from parents who were selected based upon their genetic disease profile. The puppies' mother should have been vaccinated, free of all internal and external parasites and properly nourished. For these reasons, a visit to the veterinarian who cared for the dam

Did You Know?

Obesity is linked to the earlier onset of age-related health problems. Keep weight in line by providing sufficient exercise and play, and by feeding proper serving sizes. Because calorie requirements decline as your puppy reaches adulthood and can drop 25 to 30 percent within a couple of months after spaying/neutering, you'll probably need to reduce serving portions and switch to a less calorie-dense diet.

(mother) is recommended if at all possible. The dam passes disease resistance to her puppies, which should last from 8 to 10 weeks. Unfortunately, she can also pass on parasites and infection. This is why knowing

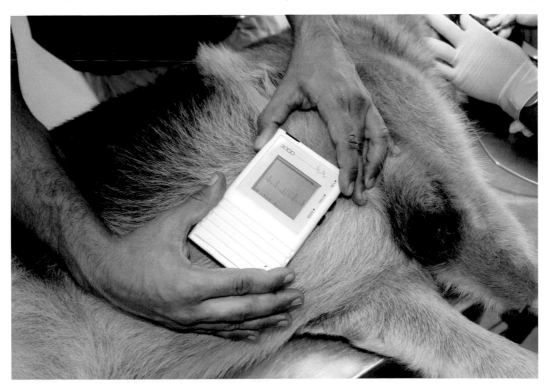

about her health is useful in learning more about the health of her puppies.

Now that you have your GSD puppy home safe and sound, it's time to arrange your pup's first trip to the veterinarian. Perhaps the breeder can recommend someone in the area who specializes in German Shepherd Dogs, or maybe you know other GSD owners who can suggest a good vet. Either way, you should make an appointment within a couple of days of bringing home your puppy. If possible, see if you can stop for this first vet appointment before going home.

The pup's first vet visit will consist of an overall examination to make sure that your pup does not have any problems that are not apparent to you. The veterinarian also will set up a schedule for the pup's vaccinations; the breeder should inform you of which ones your puppy has already received, and the vet can continue from there.

Your puppy also will have his teeth examined and have his skeletal conformation and general health checked prior to certification by the veterinarian. Puppies in certain breeds have problems with their kneecaps, cataracts and other eye problems, heart murmurs and undescended testicles. They may also have behavioral problems, which your veterinarian can evaluate if he or she has had relevant training.

VACCINATION SCHEDULING

Most vaccinations are given by injection and should only be given by a veterinarian. Both you and the vet should keep a record of the date of the injection, the identification of the vaccine and the amount given. Some vets give a first vaccination at 8 weeks of age, but most dog breeders prefer the course not to commence until about 10 weeks because of interaction with the antibodies produced by the mother. The vaccination

scheduling is usually based on a 15-day cycle. You must take your vet's advice as to when to vaccinate, as this may differ according to the vaccine used.

The usual vaccines contain immunizing doses of several different viruses such as distemper, parvovirus, parainfluenza and hepatitis. There are other vaccines available when the puppy is at a greater risk for viral exposures. You should rely on your vet's advice. This is especially true for the booster immunizations. Most vaccination programs

Set up a vet visit before you even bring your new dog home, so you can interview the veterinary staff.

Check with your vet about booster immunizations for your growing GSD puppy.

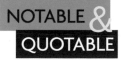

NOTABLE & QUOTABLE *GSDs are prone to gastrointestinal problems usually resulting in soft, unformed or watery stools. Keeping these problems under control is important.*

— Tony Cherubini, a German Shepherd breeder from Newberry, S.C.

Smart owners won't pick just any vet out of the phone book; they will invest time in researching and interviewing the best vet for their dog.

require a booster when the puppy is a year old and once a year thereafter. In some cases, circumstances may require more frequent immunizations.

Kennel cough, more formally known as *tracheobronchitis*, is combatted with a vaccine that is sprayed into the dog's nostrils. Kennel cough is usually included in routine vaccinations, but it is often not as effective as the vaccines for other major diseases.

Your veterinarian probably will recommend that your German Shepherd puppy be fully vaccinated before you take him on outings. There are airborne diseases, parasite eggs in the grass and unexpected visits from other dogs that might be dangerous to your puppy's health. Other dogs are the most

harmful reservoir of pathogenic organisms, as everything they have can be transmitted to your puppy.

6 Months to 1 Year of Age: Unless you intend to breed or show your dog, neutering or spaying your GSD at 6 months of age is recommended. Discuss this with your veterinarian. Neutering and spaying have proven to be beneficial to male and female puppies, respectively. Besides eliminating the possibility of pregnancy, it inhibits (but does not prevent) breast cancer in females and prostate cancer in male dogs.

Your veterinarian should provide your GSD puppy with a thorough dental evaluation at 6 months of age, ascertaining whether all his permanent teeth have

GSDs are big dogs with big responsibilities. These dogs are from working lines. They have a high drive and high energy; they need to be with you; they are very smart and very engaging; they do not make good couch potatoes. A German Shepherd will not be happy if he is not a member of the family. — Patty Visser, a volunteer with Mid-Atlantic German Shepherd Rescue in Maryland

When selecting a vet for your dog, make sure he or she is familiar with German Shepherd Dogs.

GSDs Rock

We Love German Shepherd Dogs

erupted properly. A home dental care regimen should be initiated at 6 months, including weekly brushing and providing good dental devices (such as nylon bones). Regular dental care promotes healthy teeth, fresh breath and a longer life.

Dogs Older Than 1 Year: Continue to visit the veterinarian at least once a year as bodily functions do change with age. The eyes and ears are no longer as efficient. Liver, kidney and intestinal functions often decline. Proper dietary changes recommended by your veterinarian can make life more pleasant for your aging GSD and you.

EVERYDAY HAPPENINGS

Keeping your German Shepherd Dog healthy is a matter of keen observation and quick action when necessary. Knowing what's normal for your dog will help you recognize signs of trouble before they blossom into a full-blown emergency situation.

Even if the problem is minor, such as a cut or scrape, you'll want to care for it immediately to prevent infection, as well as to ensure that your dog doesn't make it worse by chewing or scratching at it. Here's what to do for common, minor injuries or illnesses, and how to recognize and deal with emergencies.

Stay on top of your dog's health by keeping a record of his vaccinations.

Just like with infants, puppies need a series of vaccinations to ensure that they stay healthy during their first year of life. Download a vaccination chart from **DogChannel.com/Club-GSD** that you can fill out for your German Shepherd Dog.

Cuts and Scrapes: For a cut or scrape that's half an inch or smaller, clean the wound with saline solution or warm water and use tweezers to remove any splinters or other debris. Apply an antibiotic ointment. No bandage is necessary unless the wound is on a paw, which can pick up dirt when your dog walks on it. Deep cuts with lots of bleeding or those caused by glass or some other object should be treated by your veterinarian.

Cold Symptoms: Dogs don't actually get colds, but they can get illnesses that have similar symptoms, such as coughing, a runny nose or sneezing. Dogs cough for any number of reasons, from respiratory infections to inhaled irritants to congestive heart failure. Take your GSD to the veterinarian for prolonged coughing, or coughing accompanied by labored breathing, runny eyes and nose, or bloody phlegm.

A runny nose that continues for more than several hours requires veterinary attention, as well. If your GSD sneezes, he may have some mild nasal irritation that will resolve on its own, but frequent sneezing, especially if it's accompanied by a runny nose, may indicate anything from allergies to an infection or something stuck in his nose.

Vomiting and Diarrhea: Sometimes dogs can suffer minor gastric upset when they eat a new type of food, eat too much, eat the contents of the trash can or become excited or anxious. Give your German Shepherd Dog's stomach a rest by withholding food for 12 hours, and then feeding him a bland diet such as baby food or rice and chicken, gradually returning your dog to his normal food. Projectile vomiting, vomiting or diarrhea that continues for more than 48 hours, is another matter. If this happens, immediately take your German Shepherd to the veterinarian.

MORE HEALTH HINTS

A German Shepherd Dog's anal glands can cause problems if not periodically evacuated. In the wild, dogs regularly clear their anal glands to mark their territory, but in domestic dogs this function is no longer necessary; thus, their contents can build up and clog, causing discomfort. Signs that the anal glands — located on both sides of the anus — need emptying are if a GSD drags his rear end along the ground or keeps turning around to lick the area of discomfort.

While care must be taken not to cause injury, anal glands can be evacuated by pressing gently on either side of the anal opening and by using a piece of cotton or a tissue to collect the foul-smelling matter. If anal glands are allowed to become impacted, abscesses can form, causing pain and the need for veterinary attention.

GSDs can get into all sorts of mischief, so it is not uncommon for them to swallow something poisonous in the course of their investigations. Obviously, an urgent visit to your vet is required under such circumstances, but if possible, when you telephone your vet, you should inform him which poisonous substance has been ingested, because different treatments are needed. Should it be necessary to cause your dog to vomit (which is not always the case with poisoning), a small lump of baking soda, given orally, will have an immediate effect. Alternatively, a small teaspoon of salt or mustard, dissolved in water, will have a similar effect but may be more difficult to administer and take longer to work.

German Shepherd puppies often have painful fits while they are teething. These are not usually serious and are brief. Of course, you must be certain that the cause is nothing more than teething. Giving a puppy something hard to chew on usually will solve this temporary problem.

Prevention is the best medicine. Keep your GSD active and you can avoid many health complications.

The German Shepherd Dog excels in just about everything! This breed has long been prized across the globe for his intelligence, versatility, loyalty and working capabilities, as well as his natural athleticism, sensitivity and desire to please. These attributes allow the GSD to consistently excel in guiding, police work, search and rescue, herding and, not least of all, being a devoted family companion.

Ironically, along with the genes that yield such a magnificent animal, the German Shepherd Dog, like all animals, also carries the genes for hereditary diseases. Among the more serious genetic diseases that trouble this breed are degenerative myelopathy, exocrine pancreatic insufficiency, bloat, and hip and elbow dysplasia.

DEGENERATIVE MYELOPATHY

Degenerative myelopathy is a slow, progressive disease of the thoracolumbar spinal cord, the part of the spinal cord that tells the brain where the hind legs are. Although DM is seen in many breeds, it's especially common in German Shepherds.

Initial signs of DM are progressive hind limb incoordination. Affected dogs don't know where their hind legs are, and thus cannot move them correctly. Eventually,

Did You Know?

Dogs can get many diseases from ticks, including Lyme disease, Rocky Mountain spotted fever, tick bite paralysis and many others.

the disease progresses to the point that the German Shepherd falls. A myelogram (an X-ray of the spine after dye has been injected) or an MRI scan can help rule out diseases that cause similar symptoms, but often DM is a best-guess diagnosis based on the dog's history and a physical exam.

For most cases, no treatment is effective. "There is nothing that will guarantee stabilization of the condition, with the possible exception of some of those few dogs that are pathologically vitamin B-12 or vitamin E deficient," says veterinarian David A. Williams, who is department head of small animal medicine and surgery at Texas A&M University. "People recommend various things, but there is no proof that they make a difference. Similarities to multiple sclerosis support the idea that DM may be an immune-mediated disease, but there is no conclusive evidence to support that."

Williams notes that because of the German Shepherd's size, the use of a paraplegic cart to provide some mobility for affected dogs is difficult. "I wouldn't say it's impossible, but the owners I've known that have tried to manage these dogs in this way have been very discouraged and upset by the whole process," he says.

For those dogs whose myelopathy is related to vitamin E or vitamin B-12 deficiency, supplementation with vitamin E or vitamin B-12 may stabilize and even slightly improve the disease.

EXOCRINE PANCREATIC INSUFFICIENCY

Exocrine pancreatic insufficiency is a disease of the pancreas in which the cells that produce the digestive enzymes are destroyed by disease. As a result, dogs can no longer digest and absorb food. Untreated dogs suffer from progressive starvation and die. However, with treatment, the disease is usually well-managed, and affected dogs go on to live otherwise normal lives.

Evidence suggests that these animal are born with a normal pancreas. Then, usually between 1 and 5 years of age, the pancreatic cells begin to disappear. Although lots of other breeds also get EPI, the German Shepherd is over-represented. About 40 percent of cases diagnosed are German Shepherds, and it's the same around the world. In England, 40 to 60 percent of cases seen are German Shepherds.

The first signs an owner might see in a dog suffering from EPI is flatulence, rumbling intestinal sounds, lack of appetite, gradual weight loss and changes in the dog's stool. Fortunately, diagnosis can be made through a blood test. Even better, treatment is simple: Just mix pancreatic enzymes into the dog's food.

CHRONIC HIP DYSPLASIA

Chronic hip dysplasia results in a loose hip joint and abnormal rubbing of the joint surfaces. The joint eventually becomes inflamed, causing chronic pain and even the development of arthritis.

The most common heritable orthopedic disease in dogs, chronic hip dysplasia is the No. 1 genetic health problem in dogs, and the German Shepherd Dog is no exception.

Clinical signs of hip dysplasia include limping, difficulty getting up, stiffness, altered gait, struggling to go up stairs or get into the car, and reduced interest in play. Treatment options vary depending upon the type of symptoms your dog experiences, his age and when he is diagnosed. Conservative treatments for mildly dysplastic dogs include:

● weight control. Shedding extra pounds is often enough to decrease or eliminate joint pain in dogs.

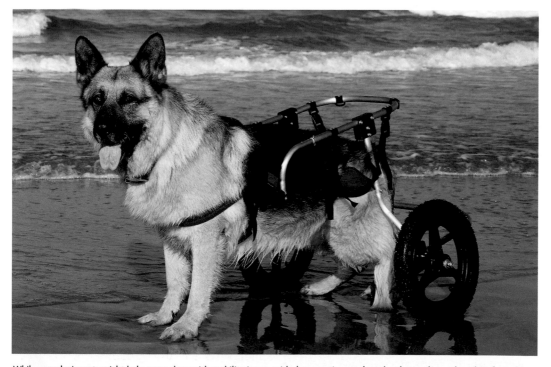

While paraplegic carts might help some dogs with mobility issues, with degenerative myelopathy, the results are less than favorable.

● prescription diets to help improve joint function. Choose a formula that contains omega-3 fatty acids for best results. Some of these formulas also contain glucosamine and chondroitin, although the amounts may not be adequate, according to Darryl Millis, D.V.M., who is also a professor of orthopedic surgery at the University of Tennessee, Knoxville. "These diets replace the need for separate supplementation with omega-3 fatty acids," Millis says.

● glucosamine/chondroitin supplements to promote joint health (if not provided in adequate amounts in your German Shepherd's formula). Studies in arthritic humans found that glucosamine/chondroitin supplements helped those with moderate to severe knee pain However, well-controlled, long-term studies are still needed in clinically affected animals.

● pain-relief drugs (anti-inflammatories prescribed under veterinary supervision). Some dogs show better results with one medication over another, so you may have to try a couple of different types before finding one that works best for your dog.

● regular exercise to maintain muscle tone, strength and range of motion in the joint. Regular, low-impact activity such as swimming or leash walks at a speed and distance your dog can handle (not to the point of lameness or stiffness) are recommended. Another good exercise is "dancing" the dog frontward. "Pick up the dog's forelimbs and walk him forward as you walk backward," Millis explains. "This strengthens the gluteal muscles and helps reduce arthritis pain. But don't walk the dog backward, as this could cause hip pain because of the more extended position of the hip joint."

● TENS (transcutaneous electrical nerve stimulation), a device that uses electrical impulse to reduce pain. "We found positive response to that," Millis says. "Most treatments last 20 to 30 minutes."

● ESWT (extracorporeal shockwave therapy), a treatment that uses sound waves to induce pain relief. "We tested dogs who were pretty bad and found, in general, a single treatment lasted several months," Millis says. Studies elsewhere found that less severely affected dogs achieved pain relief for up to two years.

More severely affected dogs as well as young dogs may best be served by surgical procedures. Surgical options include:

▲ JPS (juvenile pubic symphysidesis). If diagnosed before a puppy reaches 14 to 16 weeks of age, this simple, minimally invasive procedure can be performed, often in combination with an early spay or neuter. With this procedure, growing cartilage cells in the lower pelvis are cauterized to create a tighter hip joint. "Most puppies aren't symptomatic by that age," Millis notes, "but for high-risk dogs or loose-hipped puppies, it may be beneficial to perform JPS prophylactically during a spay or neuter."

Many canine skin irritations can be avoided or reduced by employing a simple preventive regimen:

■ Keep your GSD's skin clean and dry.
■ Shampoo your dog regularly (especially during allergy season) with a hypoallergenic shampoo.
■ Rinse the coat thoroughly.
■ Practice good flea control.
■ Supplement your dog's diet with fatty acids, such as omega-3.

▲ TPO (triple pelvic osteotomy). The pelvic bone is cut in three places and repositioned to better secure the hip femoral head. "TPO is best performed in growing dogs with minimal or no arthritic changes," Millis states. "It doesn't work as well after arthritic changes have occurred. That's a mistake some dog owners make: They adopt a wait-and-see attitude and in as little as two to four weeks, they lose their window of opportunity for that procedure."

▲ femoral head and neck incision. Best for dogs weighing less than 50 pounds, this technique removes the femoral head and neck, forming a false joint.

▲ hip replacement surgery. Although expensive, hip replacement surgery provides your dog with a functional, albeit artificial hip. "Many dogs with a hip replacement have a profound improvement in their quality of their life," Millis reports.

Prognosis varies, depending upon treatment options and the severity of the disease. Mildly affected dogs can often be successfully managed with conservative treatments for a long time. The outlook for hip repair and reconstruction generally ranges from good to excellent.

Although hip dysplasia is a genetic disorder, other causes include overfeeding and over- or under-supplementation of carbohydrates, calcium and phosphorous in growing dogs. Talk with your veterinarian to find the appropriate diet formula for your puppy or adolescent dog.

LUXATED PATELLA

A slipped kneecap (*patellar luxation*) occurs when the patella (a flat, movable bone at the front of the knee) pops out of place. A common hereditary disorder, luxated patellas usually affect knee joints and tend to strike dogs 6 months old or younger,

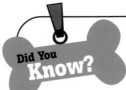

Did You **Know?**

Across the globe, more than 800 species of ticks exist, and they aren't particular to where they dine. Mammals, birds and reptiles are all fair game.

although dogs can be older when the disorder is first noticed. Trauma to the knee can also force the patella out of place.

The common sign is when the rear lower leg seems to momentarily lock, causing a skipping or hopping gait. In mild cases, the patella drops back into place again, but in more serious cases, the luxation occurs more frequently for longer periods with the dog exhibiting lameness or discomfort.

Mild cases of occasional luxations without residual lameness don't need treatment, although monitoring and veterinary evaluation are important in case the luxation worsens. Otherwise, dogs with more frequent or extended luxations, or those exhibiting lameness or discomfort, should undergo surgical correction soon after diagnosis to avoid worsening joint damage and preventing permanent lameness.

When treated promptly, prognosis for a full recovery is usually good. Keep in mind that the more damage the patella joint undergoes, the more difficult and expensive it is to repair the abnormalities and to achieve complete surgical correction.

PARASITE BITES

Insect bites itch, erupt and can become infected. Dogs have the same reaction to fleas, ticks and mites. When an insect lands on you, you can whisk it away. Unfortunately, when your GSD is bitten by a flea, tick or mite, he can only scratch or bite.

By the time your GSD has been bitten, the parasite has done its damage. It also may have laid eggs, which will cause further problems. The itching from parasite bites is probably due to the saliva injected into the site when the parasite sucks the dog's blood.

AIRBORNE ALLERGIES

Just as humans suffer from hay fever during the pollen season, many dogs suffer from the same allergies. When the pollen count is high, your GSD might suffer, but don't expect him to sneeze or have a runny nose like a human. German Shepherds react to pollen allergies in the same way they react to fleas; they scratch and bite themselves. Dogs, like humans, can be tested for allergens. Be sure to discuss allergy testing with your vet.

AUTO-IMMUNE ILLNESS

An auto-immune illness is one in which the immune system overacts and does not recognize parts of the affected person. Instead, the immune system starts to react as if these parts were foreign cells and need to be destroyed. An example of an auto-immune illness is rheumatoid arthritis, which occurs when the body does not recognize the joints. This leads to a very painful and damaging reaction in the joints. Rheumatoid arthritis has nothing to do with age, so it can also occur in puppies. The wear-and-tear arthritis in older people or dogs is called osteoarthritis.

Lupus is another auto-immune disease that affects dogs as well as people. It can take variable forms, affecting the kidneys, bones and the skin. It can be fatal, so it is treated with steroids, which have very significant side effects. Steroids calm down the allergic reaction to the body's tissues, which helps the lupus, but also affects the body's reaction to actual foreign cells such as bacteria, and also thins the skin and bones.

Purchasing your German Shepherd from a reputable breeder will greatly increase your chances of having a dog who will live a long, healthy life.

FOOD ALLERGIES

Feeding your German Shepherd Dog properly is very important. An incorrect diet could affect your dog's health, behavior and nervous system, possibly making a normal dog an aggressive one. The result of a good or bad diet is most visible in a dog's skin and coat, but internal organs are affected, too.

Dogs are allergic to many foods that are popular and highly recommended by breeders and veterinarians. Changing the brand of food may not eliminate the problem if the ingredient to which your dog is allergic is contained in the new brand.

Recognizing a food allergy can be difficult. Humans often have rashes or swelling of the lips or eyes when they eat foods they are allergic to. Dogs do not usually develop rashes, but they react the same way they do to an airborne or bite allergy; they itch, scratch and bite. While pollen allergies and parasite bites are usually seasonal, food allergies are year-round problems.

Diagnosis of a food allergy is based on a two- to four-week dietary trial with a home-cooked diet, excluding all other foods. The diet should consist of boiled rice or potato with a source of protein that your GSD has never eaten before, such as fresh or frozen fish, lamb or even something as exotic as pheasant. Water has to be the only drink, and it is important that no other foods are fed during this trial. If your dog's condition improves, try the original diet again to see if the itching resumes. If it does, then your dog is allergic to his original diet. You must find a diet that does not distress your dog's skin. Start with a commercially available hypoallergenic food or the homemade diet that you created for the allergy trial.

Food intolerance is the inability to completely digest certain foods. This occurs

SMART TIP!

Brush your dog's teeth every day. Plaque colonizes on the tooth surface in as little as six to eight hours, and if not removed by brushing, forms calculus (tartar) within three to five days. Plaque and tartar cause gum disease, periodontal disease, loosening of the teeth and tooth loss. In bad cases of dental disease, bacteria from the mouth can get into the bloodstream, leading to kidney or heart problems — all of which are life-shortening problems.

because the dog does not have the enzymes necessary to digest some foodstuffs. All puppies have the enzymes needed to digest canine milk, but some dogs do not have the enzymes to digest cow milk, resulting in loose bowels, stomach pains and flatulence.

Dogs often do not have the enzymes to digest soy or other beans. The treatment is to exclude these foods from your GSD's diet.

EXTERNAL PARASITES

Fleas: Of all the health and grooming problems to which canines are susceptible, none is better known and more frustrating than fleas. Flea infestation is relatively simple to cure but difficult to prevent.

To control flea infestation, you have to understand the flea's life cycle. Fleas are often thought of as a summertime problem, but centrally heated homes have made fleas a year-round problem. The most effective method of flea control is a two-stage approach: kill the adult fleas, then control the development of pre-adult (pupae) fleas. Unfortunately, no single active ingredient is effective against all stages of the flea life cycle.

Treating fleas should be a two-pronged attack. First, the environment needs to be treated; this includes carpets and furniture, especially your GSD's bedding and areas underneath furniture. The environment should be treated with a household spray containing an insect growth regulator and an insecticide to kill the adult fleas. Most insecticides are effective against eggs and larvae; they actually mimic the fleas' own hormones and stop the eggs and larvae from developing into adult fleas. There are currently no treatments available to attack the pupae stage of the life cycle, so the adult insecticide is used to kill the newly hatched adult fleas before they find a host. Most insect growth regulators are active for many months, while adult insecticides are only active for a few days.

When treating fleas with a household spray, vacuum before applying the product. This stimulates as many pupae as possible to hatch into adult fleas. The vacuum cleaner should also be treated with an insecticide to prevent the eggs and larvae that have been collected in the vacuum bag from hatching.

The second stage of treatment is to apply an adult insecticide to your German Shepherd Dog. Traditionally, this would be in the form of a collar or a spray, but more recent innovations include digestible insecticides that poison the fleas when they ingest the dog's blood. Alternatively, there are drops that, when placed on the back of the dog's neck, spread throughout the hair and skin to kill adult fleas.

Ticks: Though not as common as fleas, ticks are found all over the tropical and temperate world. They don't bite like fleas; they harpoon. They dig their sharp *proboscis* (nose) into your German Shepherd's skin and drink the blood, which is their only food and drink. Ticks are controlled the same way fleas are controlled.

The American dog tick, *Dermacentor variabilis,* may be the most common dog tick in many areas, especially those areas where the climate is hot and humid. Most dog ticks have life expectancies of a week to 6 months, depending on climatic conditions. They can neither jump nor fly, but they can crawl slowly and can range up to 16 feet to reach a sleeping or unsuspecting dog.

Mites: Just as fleas and ticks can be problematic for your dog, mites can also lead to an itch fit. Microscopic in size, mites are related to ticks and generally take up permanent residence on their host animal — in this case, your GSD. The term "mange" refers to any infestation caused by one of the mighty mites, of which there are six varieties that smart dog owners should know about.

■ Demodex mites cause a condition known as *demodicosis* (sometimes called "red mange" or "follicular mange"), in which the mites live in the dog's hair follicles and sebaceous glands in larger-than-normal numbers. Most dogs recover from this type of mange without any treatment, though topical therapies are commonly prescribed by the veterinarian.

■ The *Cheyletiellosis* mite is the hookmouthed culprit associated with "walking dandruff," a condition that affects dogs as well as cats and rabbits. If untreated, this mange can affect a whole kennel of dogs and can be spread to humans as well.

■ The Sarcoptes mite causes intense itching on the dog in the form of a condition known as scabies or sarcoptic mange. Scabies is highly contagious and can be passed to humans. Sometimes an allergic reaction to the mite worsens the severe itching associated with sarcoptic mange.

■ Ear mites, *Otodectes cynotis*, lead to otodectic mange, which commonly affects the outer ear canal of the dog, though other areas can be affected as well. Your vet can prescribe a treatment to flush out the ears and kill any eggs in the ears. A complete month of treatment is necessary to cure this mange.

■ Two other mites, less common in dogs, include *Dermanyssus gallinae* (the "poultry" or "red mite") and *Eutrombicula alfreddugesi* (the North American mite associated with trombiculidiasis or chigger infestation). The types of mange caused by both of these mites must be treated by vets.

INTERNAL PARASITES

Most animals — fish, birds and mammals, including dogs and humans — have worms and other parasites that live inside their bodies. According to Dr. Herbert R. Axelrod, a fish pathologist, there are two kinds of parasites: "dumb" and "smart." The smart parasites live in peaceful cooperation with their hosts — a symbiotic relationship — while the dumb parasites kill their hosts. Most worm infections are relatively easy to control. If they are not controlled, they weaken the host dog to the point that other medical problems occur, but they do not kill the host as dumb parasites would.

Roundworms: Roundworms that infect dogs live in the dog's intestines and shed eggs continually. It has been estimated that a dog produces about six or more ounces of feces every day. Each ounce averages hundreds of thousands of roundworm eggs. There are no known areas in which dogs roam that do not contain roundworm eggs.

Because roundworms infect people, too, it is wise to have your dog regularly tested.

Roundworm infection can kill puppies and cause severe problems in adult dogs, as the hatched larvae travel to the lungs and trachea through the bloodstream. Cleanliness is the best prevention against roundworms. Always pick up after your dog and dispose of feces in appropriate receptacles.

Hookworms: Hookworms are dangerous to humans as well as to dogs and cats, and can be the cause of severe anemia due to iron deficiency. The worm uses its teeth to attach itself to the dog's intestines and changes the site of its attachment about six times per day. Each time the worm repositions itself, the dog loses blood and can become anemic.

Symptoms of hookworm infection include dark stools, weight loss, general weakness, pale coloration and anemia, as well as possible skin problems. Fortunately, hookworms are easily purged with a number of medications that have proven effective. Discuss these with your veterinarian. Most heart-

worm preventives include a hookworm insecticide, as well.

Humans, can be infected by hookworms through exposure to contaminated feces. Because the worms cannot complete their life cycle on a human, the worms simply infest the skin and cause irritation. As a preventive, use disposable gloves or a poop scoop to pick up your dog's droppings and prevent your dog (or neighborhood cats) from defecating in children's play areas.

Tapeworms: There are many species of tapeworms, all of which are carried by fleas! Fleas are so small that your GSD could pass them onto your hands, your plate or your food, making it possible for you to ingest a flea that is carrying tapeworm eggs. While tapeworm infection is not life-threatening in dogs (it's a smart parasite!), it can be the cause of a serious liver disease in humans.

Whipworms: In North America, whipworms are counted among the most common parasitic worms in dogs. Affected dogs may only experience upset tummies, colic and diarrhea. These worms, however, can live for months or years in the dog, beginning their larval stage in the small intestine, spending their adult life in the large intestine and finally passing infective eggs through the dog's feces. The only way to detect whipworms is through a fecal examination, though this is not always foolproof. Treatment for whipworms is tricky, due to the worms' unusual life cycle, and often dogs are reinfected due to exposure to infective eggs on the ground. Cleaning up droppings in your backyard and in public places is necessary for sanitary purposes and the health of your dog and others.

Threadworms: Though less common than roundworms, hookworms and the aforemetioned parasites, threadworms concern dog owners in the southwestern

United States and the Gulf Coast area where the climate is hot and humid.

Living in the small intestine of the dog, this worm measures a mere two millimeters and is round in shape. Like the whipworm, the threadworm's life cycle is very complex and the eggs and larvae are tansported through the feces.

A deadly disease in humans, threadworms readily infect people, mostly through the handling of feces. Threadworms are most often seen in young puppies. The most common symptoms include bloody diarrhea and pneumonia. Sick puppies must be isolated and treated immediately; vets recommend a follow-up treatment one month later.

Heartworms: Heartworms are thin, extended worms that measure up to 12 inches long and live in a dog's heart and the major blood vessels aound it. Dogs may have up to 200 heartworms. Symptoms may be loss of energy, loss of appetite, coughing, the development of a pot belly and anemia.

Heartworms are transmitted by mosquitoes, which drink the blood of infected dogs and take in larvae with the blood. The larvae, called *microfilariae*, develop within the body of the mosquito and are then passed on to the next dog bitten after the larvae mature.

It takes two to three weeks for the larvae to develop to the infective stage within the body of the mosquito. Dogs are usually treated at about 6 weeks of age and maintained on a prophylactic dose given monthly.

Blood testing for heartworms is not necessarily indicative of how seriously your dog is infected. Although this is a dangerous disease, it is difficult for a dog to be infected. Discuss the various preventives with your vet, because there are many different types now available. Together you can decide on a safe course of prevention for your dog.

Fleas don't have to be part of your dog's life. Use prevention techniques to keep him flea free.

You have probably heard it a thousand times: You are what you eat. Believe it or not, it is very true. For dogs, they are what you feed them because they have little choice in the matter. Even smart owners who want to feed their GSDs the best often cannot do so because it can be so confusing. With the overwhelming assortment of dog foods, it's difficult to figure out which one is truly best for their dogs.

BASIC TYPES

Dog foods are produced in various types: dry, wet (canned), semimoist and frozen.

Dry food is useful for cost-conscious owners because it tends to be less expensive than the others. These foods also contain the least fat and the most preservatives. Dry food is bulky and takes longer to eat than other foods, so it's more filling.

Wet food — available in cans or foil pouches — is usually 60 to 70 percent water and is more expensive than dry food. A palatable source of concentrated nutrition, wet food also makes a good supplement for underweight dogs or those recovering from illnesses. Some owners add a little wet food to dry food to increase its appeal.

it's a
Fact

Bones can cause gastro-intestinal obstruction and perforation, and may be contaminated with salmonella or E. coli. Leave them in the trash and give your dog a nylon bone toy instead.

Semimoist food is flavorful, but it usually contains lots of sugar. That can lead to dental problems and obesity. Therefore, semimoist food is not a good choice for your German Shepherd Dog's main diet.

Likewise, **frozen food**, which is available in cooked and in raw forms, is usually more expensive than wet foods. The advantages of frozen food are similar to those of wet foods.

The amount of food that your GSD needs depends on a number of factors, such as his age, activity level, the quality of the food, reproductive status (if your German Shepherd is a female) and size. What's the easiest way to figure it out? Start with the manufacturer's recommended amount, then adjust it according to your dog's response. For example, feed the recommended amount for a few weeks, and if your GSD loses weight, increase the amount by 10 to 20 percent. If your shepherd gains weight, decrease the amount. It won't take long to determine the amount of food that keeps your best friend in optimal condition.

NUTRITION 101

All shepherds (and all dogs, for that matter) need proteins, carbohydrates, fats, vitamins and minerals to be in peak condition.

■ **Proteins** are used for growth and repair of muscles, bones and other tissues. They're also used for the production of antibodies, enzymes and hormones. All dogs need protein, but it's especially important for puppies because they grow and develop so quickly. Protein sources include various types of meat, meat meal, meat byproducts, eggs, dairy products and soybeans.

■ **Carbohydrates** are metabolized into glucose, the body's principal energy source. Carbohydrates are available as sugars, starches and fiber.

• Sugars (simple carbohydrates) are not suitable nutrient sources for dogs.

• Starches — a preferred carbohydrate in dog food — are found in a variety of plant products. Starches must be cooked in order to be digested.

• Fiber (cellulose) — also a preferred type of carbohydrate found in dog food — isn't digestible, but helps the digestive tract function properly.

■ **Fats** are also a source of energy and play an important role in maintaining your GSD's skin and coat health, hormone production, nervous system function and vitamin transport. However, you must be aware of the fact that fats increase the palatability and the calorie count of dog food, which can lead to serious health problems, such as obesity, for puppies or

A healthy dog needs access to plenty of fresh, clean water all day long.

Believe it or not, during your GSD's lifetime, you'll buy a few thousand pounds of dog food! Go to **DogChannel.com/Club-GSD** and download a chart that outlines the cost of dog food.

dogs who are allowed to overindulge. Some foods contain added amounts of omega fatty acids such as docosohexaenoic acid, a compound that may enhance brain development and learning in puppies but is not considered an essential nutrient by the Association of American Feed Control Officials (www.aafco.org). Fats used in dog foods include tallow, lard, poultry fat, fish oil and vegetable oils.

■ **Vitamins** and **minerals** are essential to dogs for proper muscle and nerve function, bone growth, healing, metabolism and fluid balance. Especially important for your German Shepherd puppy are calcium, phosphorus and vitamin D, which must be supplied in the right balance to ensure proper development and maintenance of bones and teeth.

Just as your dog receives proper nutrition from his food, water is an essential nutrient, as well. Water keeps your dog's body hydrated and facilitates normal function of the body's systems. During housetraining, it is necessary to keep an eye on how much water your German Shepherd Dog is drinking, but once he is reliably trained, he should have access to clean, fresh water at all times, especially if you feed him dry food. Make sure that your dog's water bowl is clean, and change the water often.

CHECK OUT THE LABEL

To help you get a feel for what you are feeding your dog, start by taking a look at the label on the package or can. Look for the words "complete and balanced." This tells you that the food meets specific nutritional requirements set by the AAFCO for either adults ("maintenance") or puppies and pregnant/lactating females ("growth and reproduction"). The label must state the group for which the food is intended. If you're feeding

Dogs of all ages love treats and table food, but these goodies can unbalance your German Shepherd's diet and lead to a weight problem if you don't feed him wisely. Table food, whether fed as a treat or as part of a meal, shouldn't account for more than 10 percent of your dog's daily caloric intake. If you plan to give your GSD treats, be sure to include "treat calories" when calculating the daily food requirement — so you don't end up with a pudgy pup!

When shopping for packaged treats, look for ones that provide complete nutrition. They're basically dog food in a fun form. Choose crunchy goodies for chewing fun and dental health. Other ideas for tasty treats include:

✓ small chunks of cooked, lean meat
✓ dry dog food morsels
✓ cheese
✓ veggies (cooked, raw or frozen)
✓ breads, crackers or dry cereal
✓ unsalted, unbuttered, plain, popped popcorn

Some foods, however, can be dangerous or even deadly to a dog. The following can cause digestive upset (vomiting or diarrhea) or fatal toxic reactions:

✗ **avocados:** if eaten in sufficient quantity these can cause gastrointestinal irritation, with vomiting and diarrhea

✗ **baby food:** may contain onion powder; does not provide balanced nutrition

✗ **chocolate:** contains methylxanthines and theobromine, caffeine-like compounds that can cause vomiting, diarrhea, heart abnormalities, tremors, seizures and death. Darker chocolates contain higher levels of the toxic compounds.

✗ **eggs, raw:** Whites contain an enzyme that prevents uptake of biotin, a B vitamin; may contain salmonella.

✗ **garlic (and related foods):** can cause gastrointestinal irritation and anemia if eaten in sufficient quantity

✗ **grapes:** can cause kidney failure if eaten in sufficient quantity (the toxic dose varies from dog to dog)

✗ **macadamia nuts:** can cause vomiting, weakness, lack of coordination and other problems

✗ **meat, raw:** may contain harmful bacteria such as salmonella or E. coli

✗ **milk:** can cause diarrhea in some puppies

✗ **onions (and related foods):** can cause gastrointestinal irritation and anemia if eaten in sufficient quantity

✗ **raisins:** can cause kidney failure if eaten in sufficient quantity (the toxic dose varies from dog to dog)

✗ **yeast bread dough:** can rise in the gastrointestinal tract, causing obstruction; produces alcohol as it rises

a puppy, choose a "growth and reproduction" food.

The nutrition label also includes a list of minimum protein, minimum fat, maximum fiber and maximum moisture content. (You won't find carbohydrate content because it's everything that isn't protein, fat, fiber and moisture.)

The nutritional analysis refers to crude protein and crude fat — amounts that have been determined in the laboratory. This analysis is technically accurate, but it does not tell you anything about digestibility: how much of the particular nutrient your GSD can actually use. For information about digestibility, contact the manufacturer (check the label for a telephone number and website address).

Virtually all commercial puppy foods exceed AAFCO's minimal requirements for protein and fat, the two nutrients most commonly evaluated when comparing foods. Protein levels in dry puppy foods usually range from about 26 to 30 percent; for canned foods, the values are about 9 to 13 percent. The fat content of dry puppy foods is about 20 percent or more; for canned foods, it's 8 percent or more. (Dry food values are larger than canned food values because dry food contains less water; the values are actually similar when compared on a dry matter basis.)

Finally, check the ingredients on the label, which lists the ingredients in descending order by weight. Manufacturers are allowed to list separately different forms of a single ingredient (e.g., ground corn and corn gluten meal). The food may contain meat byproducts, meat and bone meal, and animal fat, which probably won't appeal to you but are nutritious and safe for your puppy. Higher quality foods usually have meat or meat products near the top of the ingredient

list, but you don't need to worry about grain products as long as the label indicates that the food is nutritionally complete. Dogs are omnivores (not carnivores, as commonly believed), so all balanced dog foods contain animal and plant ingredients.

STAGES OF LIFE

When selecting your dog's diet, three stages of development must be considered: the puppy stage, the adult stage and the senior stage.

Puppy Diets: Pups instinctively want to nurse, and a normal puppy will exhibit this behavior from just a few moments following birth. Puppies should be allowed to nurse for about the first six weeks, although by the third or fourth week, the breeder will begin to introduce small portions of suitable solid food. Most breeders like to initially introduce alternate milk and meat meals, leading up to weaning time.

By the time German Shepherd puppies are 7 weeks old (or a maximum of 8), they should be fully weaned and fed solely on puppy food. Selection of the most suitable, high-quality food at this time is essential because a puppy's fastest growth rate is during the

Feeding your German Shepherd is part of your daily routine.
Take a break, and have some fun online and play "Feed the GSD,"
an exclusive game found only on **DogChannel.com/Club-GSD** —
just click on "Games."

How can you tell if your GSD is fit or fat? When you run your hands down your pal's sides from front to back, you should be able to easily feel her ribs. It's OK if you feel a little body fat (and a lot of hair), but you shouldn't feel huge fat pads. You should also be able to feel your shepherd's waist — an indentation behind the ribs.

first year of life. Seek advice about your dog's diet from your veterinarian. The frequency of meals will be reduced over time, and when a young dog has reached 10 to 12 months, he should be switched to an adult diet.

Puppy and junior diets can be well balanced for the needs of your GSD so that, except in certain circumstances, additional vitamin, mineral and protein supplements will not be required.

How often should you feed your GSD in a day? Puppies have small stomachs and high metabolic rates, so they need to eat several times a day to consume sufficient nutrients. If your puppy is younger than 3 months old, feed him four or five meals a day. When your GSD is 3 to 5 months old, decrease the number of meals to three or four. At 6 months of age, most puppies can move to an adult schedule of two meals a day.

Adult Diets: A dog is considered an adult when he has stopped growing. Rely on your

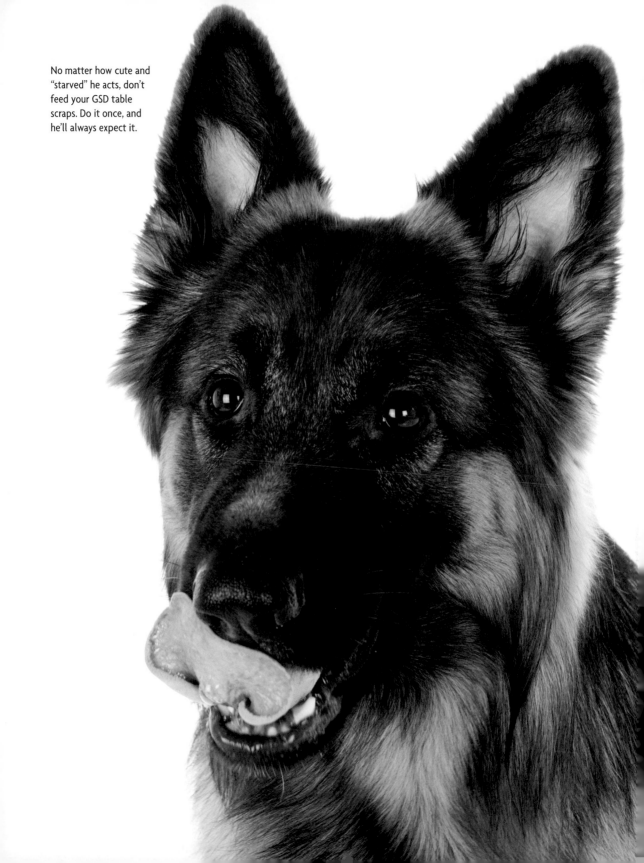

No matter how cute and "starved" he acts, don't feed your GSD table scraps. Do it once, and he'll always expect it.

veterinarian or dietary specialist to recommend an acceptable maintenance diet. Major dog food manufacturers specialize in this type of food, and smart owners must select the one best suited to their dogs' needs. Do not leave food out all day for "free-choice" feeding, as this freedom inevitably translates to inches around the dog's waist.

Senior Diets: As dogs get older, their metabolism begins to change. A senior German Shepherd Dog usually exercises less, moves more slowly and sleeps more.

This change in his lifestyle and physiological performance requires a change in diet. Because these changes take place slowly, they might not be recognizable at first. These metabolic changes increase the tendency toward obesity, requiring an even more vigilant approach to feeding. Obesity in an older dog exacerbates the health problems that already accompany old age.

As a GSD ages, few of his organs function up to par. The kidneys slow down, and the intestines become less efficient. These age-related factors are best handled with a change in diet and a change in feeding schedule to give smaller portions that are more easily digested.

There is no single best diet for an older German Shepherd. While many older dogs will do perfectly fine on light or senior diets, other dogs will do better on special premium diets such as lamb and rice. Be sensitive to your senior shepherd's diet, and this will help control other problems that may arise with your old friend.

Your German Shepherd Dog can't read the labels, so he looks to you to provide the best possible nutrition that you can afford.

These delicious, dog-friendly recipes will have your furry friend smacking her lips and salivating for more. Just remember: Treats aren't meant to replace your dog's regular meals. Give your German Shepherd snacks sparingly and continue to feed her nutritious, well-balanced meals.

Cheddar Squares
$\frac{1}{3}$ cup all-natural applesauce
$\frac{1}{3}$ cup low-fat cheddar cheese, shredded
$\frac{1}{3}$ cup water
2 cups unbleached white flour

In a medium bowl, mix all the wet ingredients. In a large bowl, mix all the dry ingredients. Slowly add all the wet ingredients to the dry mixture.

Mix well. Pour batter into a greased, 13x9x2-inch pan. Bake at 375-degrees Fahrenheit for 25 to 30 minutes. Bars are done when a toothpick inserted in the center and removed comes out clean. Cool and cut into bars. This recipe makes about 54, 1½-inch bars.

Peanut Butter Bites
3 tablespoons vegetable oil
$\frac{1}{4}$ cup smooth peanut butter, no salt or sugar
$\frac{1}{4}$ cup honey
1 ½ teaspoon baking powder
2 eggs
2 cups whole wheat flour

In a large bowl, mix all ingredients until dough is firm. If the dough is too sticky, mix in a small amount of flour. Knead dough on a lightly floured surface until firm. Roll out dough half an inch thick, and cut with cookie cutters. Put cookies on a cookie sheet half an inch apart. Bake at 350-degrees Fahrenheit for 20 to 25 minutes. When done, cookies should be firm to the touch. Turn oven off and leave cookies for one to two hours to harden. This recipe makes about 40, 2-inch-long cookies.

GROOMING GUIDE

Even a macho German Shepherd will appreciate a day at the hair dresser. Start when your dog is a puppy, brushing him with a soft brush to get him accustomed to how nice it feels. He might flop around and bite the brush at first, thinking that you're playing a game. If he's too rambunctious, put the brush away and try again when he's resting. He'll figure out soon enough that it's worth being still for!

GEAR UP

No matter what the commercials say, the ingredients you apply to your GSD's coat will not change a brittle, lifeless coat into a soft, healthy coat. The truth is that if you want your GSD to have a healthy coat, then take a close look at your dog's diet. Healthy hair and skin begins with good nutrition. A good premium dog food is the best place to start nourishing a healthy coat. Your dog's diet is not the place to economize. Purchase the best food you can afford and resist the impulse to save money at your GSD's expense. German Shepherds' skin can be sensitive, so consult your veterinarian

Did You Know?

Nail clipping can be tricky, so many dog owners leave the task for the professionals. However, if you walk your dog on concrete, you may not have to worry about it. The concrete acts like a nail file and will help keep the nails neatly trimmed.

when choosing your dog's diet. Once you've established a complete and balanced diet, you can move on to improving the coat from the outside.

In order to keep your GSD polished, you will need a few grooming essentials:

- nail clippers
- styptic powder
- cotton balls
- a pH-balanced dog shampoo
- ear powder or cleaner
- a coat conditioner
- hydrogen peroxide or baby wipes
- a pin brush — for thicker undercoat
- a bristle brush — for all-around grooming
- a slicker brush — removes shedding hair
- a shedding rake — for peak shedding time

BATH AND BRUSH

The best place to bathe your GSD is outside. Warm water will be more comfortable for your German Shepherd Dog and helps to loosen dead hair. If you do bathe him inside your house, place a nonskid mat in the tub and a strainer over the drain to catch hair. Use a hand-held sprayer.

Check the water temperature against the inside of your wrist or with your hand. Hold the hose or sprayer close to your German Shepherd's body to avoid excessive spray. If you don't have a hose attachment, use a plastic cup to scoop water and pour it over your dog.

Work from the highest point to the lowest on your GSD with the water and shampoo; use your fingers to massage the shampoo throughout the coat.

To keep water from getting into your dog's nose, hold your hand as a barrier around the nose, and let the water flow from behind his ears toward your hand, descending down to the beard.

After removing a tick, clean your dog's skin with hydrogen peroxide. If Lyme disease is common where you live, have your veterinarian test the tick. Tick preventive medication will discourage ticks from attaching and kill any that do.

— groomer Andrea Vilardi from West Paterson, N.J.

Shedding naturally occurs in the spring and fall, and for females, after each estrus (heat) cycle. It also can occur in times of illness, stress and excitement.

Rinse your GSD with a gentle flow of water until his coat feels clean and the water runs clear. You can use a coat conditioner after a bath, but use sparingly so as not to clog your dog's pores. Always follow the instructions on the bottle.

When drying your GSD's coat, use a blotting technique instead of rubbing the towel back and forth. If you use a hair dryer, test the air flow against the inside of your wrist first, then hold it about 10 to 12 inches from your dog so you don't burn him. Professional groomers prefer forced air dryers that rely on velocity, not heat.

BRUSH THAT DOG!

At the end of every coat growth cycle, hair dies and leaves the coat looking dull and lifeless until the dead hair is shed and new hair emerges. Frequent brushing speeds up the process and stimulates the hair follicles.

Regular brushing, at least once a week, also contributes to healthy skin. With an adult German Shepherd, start by removing as much dead or ready-to-shed hair as possible. Brushing the hair backward will loosen it, although your GSD may not be thrilled about this part. Then use the shedding rake or slicker brush to pull out the loose hair. Both of these brushes can scratch the skin, so be careful. A brush with large rubber bristles also can dislodge hair effectively. Once the loose hair is out, go over the coat with a pin brush or natural bristle brush.

IT'S SNOWING FUR!

All dogs shed. German Shepherds shed a lot. Shedding is controlled in large part by how much light he is exposed to. Dogs who live indoors, where the light doesn't correspond to the natural light schedule of the seasons, tend to shed year-round. Your best bet is to brush diligently, using a fur rake, shedding blade or rubber-toothed brush. A shedding blade is a flexible metal strip with dull sawtooth edges, looped together and attached by a handle. Whisk it over the coat in the direction of coat growth to remove dead hair.

Blow drying your GSD's coat with a dog dryer also helps, especially if you fingercomb the coat to loosen the follicles. Bathing in warm water can also loosen up the coat. Many products on the market claim to prevent shedding between the major spring and fall shedding seasons, but reports are mixed as to their usefulness, so be wary of these products.

Every dog needs a *paw*dicure from time to time.

Long-coated German Shepherd Dogs are rare; they require a little more grooming.

NOW EAR THIS

Look way down inside your dog's ears. Do you see just a little tan wax? That's fine; leave it.

Do you see gobs of gunk? That's not OK. If your GSD is constantly scratching his ears and shaking his head, take a close look at that gunk. Place some on a piece of black paper and look at it with a magnifying glass. If you see little white moving specks, your dog has ear mites. You'll need a veterinarian to confirm your diagnosis, so that he or she can prescribe a proper and effective treatment that won't damage your dog's ears.

If your German Shepherd Dog tilts his head and acts like his ear hurts, or if the ear appears red and swollen, it's time to see the veterinarian. You don't want to clean his ears if he's in pain or if there's a chance of a perforated eardrum.

Assuming your German Shepherd Dog just has dirty ears, cleaning them is quite simple. Quickly squeeze some of the cleaning solution into your dog's ear; if you go slowly, the solution will tickle and he'll shake it right out. Keep your hand on the base of the ear, and massage the liquid in so it squishes all around. Your GSD will shake the liquid out, flinging dissolved gunk all over the place, so you may want to do this outdoors. Wipe clean any goop hanging on the ears with a cotton ball. For really dirty ears, do this several times in the course of a week.

Don't stick cotton swabs into your German Shepherd's ears. They can irritate the skin, pack gunk more tightly or perforate the eardrum. Don't use pow-

For a bright, healthy smile, brush your dog's teeth several times a week.

ders, which will mix with the moisture and form a hard cake. Don't use hydrogen peroxide, which will leave the ear moist; and most of all, don't be overzealous in your cleaning. More problems are caused by owners stripping the ears of natural waxes than by neglecting to clean them.

MINIMAL EYE UPKEEP

Most German Shepherd Dogs have healthy eyes with few problems. Your dog may occasionally squint or tear because of an irritated cornea or foreign object. You can try flushing the eye with saline solution, which may sometimes help. Also, flush with saline solution or water if your GSD's eyes comes in contact with an irritating substance, and then check in with the veterinarian.

You can prevent tear stains by wiping the area with a moist cloth or using one of the products sold for their removal (available at pet-supply stores). They won't be noticeable on darker dogs, but light dogs may need more work to look their best. A solution of equal parts corn starch, milk of magnesia and hydrogen peroxide can remove stains if applied immediately after rinsing and left to dry. Once the solution is completely dry, brush the mixture off to lift the stains. Just be extremely cautious while working around your dog's eyes.

NAIL CLIPPING 4-1-1

The best time to clip your dog's nails is immediately after a bath because the water will have softened the nails, and your GSD may be somewhat tired-out by the bath. Nail trimming is recommended every two weeks, using nail clippers or a nail grinding tool.

Trimming nails are crucial to maintaining the German Shepherd Dog's normal foot shape. Long nails can permanently damage a dog's feet; the tight ligaments of round, arched feet will break down more quickly. If your dog's nails are clicking on the floor, they need trimming.

Your GSD should be accustomed to having his nails trimmed at an early age because it will be part of your maintenance routine throughout his life. Not only do neatly trimmed nails look nicer, but long nails can unintentionally scratch someone. Also, long nails have a better chance of ripping and bleeding, or causing your GSD's toes to spread.

Before you start clipping, make sure you can identify the "quick" in each nail (the vein in the center of each nail). It will bleed if accidentally cut, which will be painful for your dog since it contains a web of nerve endings. Keep some type of clotting agent on hand, such as a styptic pencil or styptic powder (the type used for shaving). This will quickly stop the bleeding when applied to the end of the cut nail. Do not panic if this happens, just stop the bleeding and talk soothingly to your dog. Once he has calmed down, move on to the next nail. It is better to clip a little at a time, particularly with dogs who have dark nails, where the quick isn't easily visible.

Hold your dog steady as you begin trimming his nails; you do not want him to make any sudden movements or run away. Talk to him calmly and stroke him as you clip. Holding his foot in your hand, simply take off the end of each nail in one quick clip. You can purchase nail clippers that are specifically made for dogs at pet-supply stores.

There are two predominant types of clippers. One is the guillotine clipper, which is a hole with a blade in the middle. Using this tool, squeeze the handles so that the blade meets the nail and chops it off. It sounds gruesome, and for some dogs, it is utterly intolerable. Scissor-type clippers are gentler on the nail. The important thing to make sure of is that the blades on either of these clippers are sharp. Once you are at the desired length, use a nail file to smooth the rough edges of the nails so they don't catch on carpeting or outdoor debris.

A third option is a cordless nail grinder fitted with a fine grade (100 grit) sandpaper cylinder. Stone cylinders are more prone to heat buildup and vibration. When grinding, use a low-speed (5,000 to 10,000 rpm). Hold your dog's paw firmly in one hand spreading the toes slightly apart. Touch the spinning grinder wheel to the nail tip for one or two seconds without applying pressure. Repeat if necessary to remove the nail tip protruding beyond the quick. Grinders have the added benefit of leaving nails smooth and free of

German Shepherd Dogs shed. A thorough daily brushing will help keep hair off of you, your furniture and carpet.

sharp, jagged edges that traditional nail clippers leave behind.

If the procedure becomes more than you can deal with, just remember: Groomers and veterinarians charge a nominal fee to clip nails. By using their services you won't have to see your pet glower at you for the rest of the night.

When inspecting feet, you must check not only your dog's nails but also the pads of his feet. Check to see that the pads have not become cracked and always inspect between the pads to be sure nothing has become lodged there. Depending upon the season, there may be a danger of grass seeds or thorns becoming embedded, or even tar from the road. Butter, by the way, is useful in removing tar from your German Shepherd's feet.

IT'S THE DARN TOOTH!

Like people, German Shepherd Dogs can suffer from dental disease, so experts recommend regular teeth cleanings. Daily brushing is best, but your dog will benefit from having his teeth brushed a few times a week. The teeth should be white and free of yellowish tartar, and the gums should appear healthy and pink. Gums that bleed easily when you perform dental duties may have gingivitis.

The first thing to know is that your puppy probably isn't going to want your fingers in his mouth. Desensitizing your puppy — getting him to accept that you will be looking at and touching his teeth — is the first step to overcoming his resistance. You can begin this as soon as you get your puppy, with the help of the thing that motivates dogs the most: food.

For starters, let your puppy lick some chicken, vegetable or beef broth off your finger. Then, dip your finger in broth again, and gently insert your finger in the side of your dog's mouth. Touch his side teeth and gums. Several sessions will get your puppy used to having his mouth touched.

Use a toothbrush specifically made for a dog or a fingertip brush to brush your German Shepherd's teeth. Hold his mouth with the fingers of one hand, and brush with the other. Use toothpaste formulated for dogs with delectable flavors like poultry and beef. Human toothpaste froths too much and can give your dog an upset stomach. Brush in a circular motion with the brush held at a 45-degree angle to the gum line. Be sure to get the fronts, tops and sides of each tooth.

Check the teeth for signs of plaque, tartar or gum disease, including redness, swelling, foul breath, discolored enamel near the gum line and receding gums. If you see these, immediately take your German Shepherd to the veterinarian.

REWARD A JOB WELL DONE

Rewarding your German Shepherd for behaving during grooming is the best way to ensure stress-free grooming throughout his lifetime. Bathing energizes your pet, and using the time immediately after grooming as play time is the best way to reward your GSD for a job well done. Watching your clean, healthy GSD tear from room to room in sheer joy is your reward for being a caring owner.

Six Tips for Breed Care

1. Grooming tools can be scary to some dogs, so let yours see and sniff everything at the start. Keep your beauty sessions short, too. Most shepherds don't enjoy standing still for too long.
2. Look at your dog's eyes for any discharge, and her ears for inflammation, debris or foul odor. If you notice anything that doesn't look right, immediately contact your veterinarian.
3. Choose a time to groom your dog when you don't have to rush, and assemble all of the grooming tools before you begin. This way you can focus on your dog's needs instead of having to stop in the middle of the session to search for an item.
4. Start establishing a grooming routine the day after you bring her home. A regular grooming schedule will make it easier to remember what touch-up your dog needs.
5. Proper nail care helps with your dog's gait and spinal alignment. Nails that are too long can force a dog to walk improperly. Also, too-long nails can snag and tear, causing painful injury to your German Shepherd Dog.
6. Good dental health prevents gum disease and early tooth loss. Brush your GSD's teeth daily and see a veterinarian yearly.

Six Questions to Ask a Groomer

1. Do you cage dry? Are you willing to hand dry or air dry my pet?
2. What type of shampoo are you using? Is it tearless? If not, do you have a tearless variety available for use?
3. Will you restrain my pet if she acts up during nail clipping? What methods do you use to handle difficult dogs?
4. Are you familiar with the German Shepherd Dog? Do you have any references from other GSD owners?
5. Is the shop air-conditioned during hot weather?
6. Will my dog be getting brushed or just bathed?

CHAPTER 10

TIME TO

TRAIN

Reward-based training methods — clicking and luring — instruct dogs on what to do and help them do it correctly, setting them up for success and rewards rather than mistakes and punishment. A clicker is a small, plastic device that makes a sharp clicking sound when a button is pressed. You can purchase them at any pet-supply store.

Clicker training is a precise way to mark a desired behavior so an animal knows exactly what behavior earned a reward. Using a clicker, you "charge" the clicker by clicking and giving your German Shepherd a treat several times, until he understands that the click means a treat is forthcoming. The click then becomes a secondary reinforcer. It's not the reward itself, but it will become so closely linked in your dog's mind with a reward that it has the same effect as a reward.

Next, you click the clicker when your German Shepherd does any desirable behavior. Then, you follow it up with a click and treat. The click exactly marks, more precisely than a word or gesture, the desired behavior, quickly teaching your dog which behaviors will earn rewards.

Did You Know? **The prime period for socialization is short.** Most behavior experts agree that positive experiences during the 10-week period between 4 and 14 weeks of age are vital to the development of a puppy who'll grow into an adult dog with sound temperament.

Most dogs find food rewards meaningful; GSDs are no exception as they tend to be food-motivated. This works well because positive training relies on using treats, at least initially, to encourage a dog to demonstrate a certain behavior. The treat is then given as a reward. When you reinforce desired behaviors with rewards that are valuable to your dog, you are met with happy cooperation rather than resistance.

Positive reinforcement does not necessarily equal passivity. While you are rewarding your German Shepherd's desirable behaviors, you must still manage him to be sure he isn't getting rewarded for his undesirable behaviors. Training tools, such as leashes, tethers, baby gates and crates, help keep your dog out of trouble. The use of force-free negative punishment (the dog's behavior makes a good thing go away) helps him realize there are negative consequences for inappropriate behaviors.

LEARNING SOCIAL GRACES

Now that you have done all of the preparatory work and have helped your GSD get accustomed to his new home and family, it's time for you to have some fun! Socializing your tiny pup gives you the opportunity to show off your new friend, and your GSD gets to reap the benefits of being an adorable little creature whom people will want to pet and gush over how precious he is.

Besides getting to know his new family, your puppy should be exposed to other people, animals and situations; but, of course, he must not come into close contact with dogs who you don't know well until he has had all his vaccinations. This will help him become well-adjusted as he grows up and less prone to being timid or fearful of the new things he will encounter.

Your pup's socialization began at the breeder's home, but now it is your responsibility to continue it. The socialization he receives up until he is 12 weeks of age is the most critical, as this is the time when he forms his impressions of the outside world. Be especially careful during the 8- to 10-week period, also known as the fear period. The interaction he receives during this time should be gentle and reassuring. Lack of socialization can manifest itself in fear and aggression as your German Shepherd matures. Puppies require a lot of human contact, affection, handling and exposure to other animals.

Once your German Shepherd Dog has received his necessary vaccinations, feel free to take him out and about (on his leash, of course). Walk him around the neighborhood, take him on your daily errands, let people pet him and let him meet other dogs and pets. Make sure to expose your GSD to different people — men, women, kids, babies, men with beards, teenagers with cell phones or riding skateboards, joggers, shoppers, someone in a wheelchair, a pregnant woman, etc. Make sure your GSD explores different surfaces like sidewalks, gravel and even a puddle. Positive experience is the key to building confidence. It's up to you to make sure your GSD safely discovers the world so he will be a calm, confident and well-socialized dog.

It's important that you take the lead in all socialization experiences and never put your pup in a scary or potentially harmful situation. Be mindful of your GSD's limitations. Fifteen minutes at a public market is fine; two hours at a loud outdoor concert is too much. Meeting vaccinated, tolerant and gentle older dogs is great. Meeting dogs who you don't know or trust isn't a great idea, especially if they appear very energetic, dominant or fearful. Control the situations in which you place your puppy.

The best way to socialize your puppy to a new experience is to make him think it's the best thing ever. You can do this with a lot of happy talk, enthusiasm and, yes, food. To convince your puppy that almost any experience is a blast, always carry

SMART TIP!

If your German Shepherd Dog refuses to sit with both haunches squarely beneath her and instead sits on one side or the other, she may have a physical reason for doing so. Discuss the habit with your veterinarian to be certain your dog isn't suffering from some structural problem.

treats. Consider carrying two types — a bag of his puppy chow, which you can give him when introducing him to nonthreatening experiences, and a bag of high-value, mouth-watering treats to give him when introducing him to unfamiliar experiences.

BASIC CUES

All GSDs, regardless of your training and relationship goals, need to know at least five basic good-manner behaviors: sit, down,

stay, come and heel. Here are tips for teaching your shepherd these important cues.

SIT: Every dog should learn to sit.

- Hold a treat at the end of your German Shepherd Dog's nose.
- Move the treat over his head.
- When your dog sits, click a clicker or say "Yes!"
- Feed your dog the treat.
- If your dog jumps up, hold the treat lower. If he backs up, back him into a corner and wait until he sits. Be patient. Keep your clicker handy, and click (or say "Yes!") and treat anytime he offers a sit.
- When he is able to easily offers sits, say "sit" just before he offers, so he can make the association between the word and the behavior. Add the sit cue when you know you can get the behavior. Your dog doesn't know what the word means until you repeatedly associate it with the appropriate behavior.
- When your GSD sits easily on cue, start using intermittent reinforcement by clicking some sits but not others. At first, click most sits and skip an occasional one (this is a high rate of reinforcement). Gradually make your clicks random.

DOWN: If your GSD can sit, then he can learn to lie down.

- ◆ Have your GSD sit.
- ◆ Hold the treat in front of his nose. Move it down slowly, straight toward the floor (toward his toes). If he follows all the way down, click and treat.
- ◆ If he gets stuck, move the treat down slowly. Click and treat for small movements downward — moving his head a bit lower, or inching one paw forward. Keep clicking and treating until your GSD is all the way down.

All dog sports, like agility, require that your dog knows at least the basic cues.

This training method is called "shaping" — rewarding small pieces of a behavior until your dog succeeds.

◆ If your dog stands as you move the treat toward the floor, have him sit, and move the treat even more slowly downward, shaping with clicks and treats for small, downward movements. If he stands, cheerfully say "Oops!" (which means "Sorry, no treat for that!"), have him sit and try again.

◆ If shaping isn't working, sit on the floor with your knee raised. Have your GSD sit next to you. Put your hand with the treat under your knee and lure him under your leg so he lies down and crawls to follow the treat. Click and treat!

◆ When you can lure the down easily, add the verbal cue, wait a few seconds to let your dog think, then lure him down to show him the association. Repeat until your GSD goes down on the verbal cue; then begin using intermittent reinforcement.

STAY: What good are sit and down cues if your dog doesn't stay?

▲ Start with your German Shepherd in a sit or down position.

▲ Put the treat in front of your dog's nose and keep it there.

▲ Click and reward several times while he is in position, then release him with a cue you will always use to tell him the stay is over. Common release cues are: "all done," "break," "free," "free dog," "at ease" and "OK."

▲ When your GSD will stay in a sit or down position while you click and treat, add your verbal stay cue. Say "stay," pause for a second or two, click and say "stay" again. Release.

▲ When your German Shepherd Dog is getting the idea, say "stay," whisk the treat out of sight behind your back, click the clicker and whisk the treat back. Be sure to get it all the way to his nose, so he doesn't jump up. Gradually increase the duration of the stay.

▲ When he will stay for 15 to 20 seconds, add small distractions: shuffling your feet, moving your arms, small hops. Gradually increase distractions. If your GSD makes mistakes, it means you're adding too much, too fast.

▲ When he'll stay for 15 to 20 seconds with distractions, gradually add distance. Have your German Shepherd stay, take a half-step back, click, return and treat. When he'll stay with a half-step, tell him to stay, take a full step back, click and return.

German Shepherd Dogs like to train. You just need to supply the lessons.

Behaviors are best trained by breaking them down into their simplest components, teaching those, and then linking them together to end up with the complete behavior. Keep treats small so you can reward many times without stuffing your shepherd. Remember, don't bore your GSD; avoid excessive repetition.

Always return to your dog to treat after you click, but before you release. If you always return, his stay becomes strong. If you call him to you, his stay gets weaker due to his eagerness to come to you.

COME: A reliable recall — coming when called — can be a challenging behavior to teach. It is possible, however. To succeed, you need to install an automatic response to your "come" cue — one so automatic that your GSD doesn't even stop to think when he hears it, but will spin on his heels and charge to you at full speed.

■ Start by charging a come cue the same way you charged your clicker. If your GSD already ignores the word "come," pick a different cue, like "front" or "hugs." Say your cue and feed him a bit of scrumptious treat. Repeat this until his eyes light up when he hears the cue. Now you're ready to start training.

■ With your GSD on a leash, run away several steps and cheerfully call out your charged cue. When he follows, click the clicker. Feed him a treat when he reaches you. For a more enthusiastic come, run away at full speed as you call him. When he follows at a gallop, stop running, click and give him a treat. The better your GSD gets at coming, the farther away he can be when you call him.

■ Once your German Shepherd understands the come cue, play with more people, each holding a clicker and treats. Stand a short distance apart and take turns calling and running away. Click and treat in turn as he comes to each of you. Gradually increase the distance until he comes flying to each person from a distance.

■ When you and your GSD are ready to practice in wide-open spaces, attach a long line — a 20- to 50-foot leash — to your dog, so you can get a hold of him if that taunting squirrel nearby is too much of a temptation. Then, head to a practice area where there are less tempting distractions.

HEEL: Heeling means that your dog can calmly walk beside you without pulling. It takes time and patience on your part to succeed at teaching your dog that you will not proceed unless he is walking beside you with ease. Pulling out ahead on the leash is definitely unacceptable.

● Begin by holding the leash in your left hand as your GSD sits beside your left leg. Move the loop end of the leash to your

SMART TIP!

If you begin teaching the heel cue by taking long walks and letting your dog pull you along, she may misinterpret this action as acceptable. When you pull back on the leash to counteract her pulling, she will read that tug as a signal to pull even harder!

right hand but keep your left hand short on the leash so it keeps your dog close to you.

● Say "heel" and step forward on your left foot. Keep your GSD close to you and take three steps. Stop and have your dog sit next to you in what we now call the heel position. Praise verbally, but do not touch your dog. Hesitate a moment and begin again with "heel," taking three steps and stopping, at which point your dog is told to sit again.

Your goal here is to have your dog walk those three steps without pulling on the leash. Once he will walk calmly beside you for three steps without pulling, increase the number of steps you take to five. When he will walk politely beside you while you take five steps, you can increase the length of your walk to 10 steps. Keep increasing the length of your stroll until your dog will walk beside you without pulling for as long as you want him to heel. When you stop heeling, indicate to the dog that the exercise is over by petting him and saying "OK, good dog." The "OK" is used as a release word, meaning that the exercise is finished, and he is free to relax.

● If you are dealing with a GSD who insists on pulling you around, simply put on your brakes and stand your ground until your GSD realizes that the two of you are not going anywhere until he is beside you and moving at your pace, not his. It may take some time just standing there to convince your dog that you are the leader, and you will be the one to decide on the direction and speed of your travel.

● Each time your dog looks up at you or slows down to give a slack leash between the two of you, quietly praise him and say, "Good heel. Good dog." Eventually, your GSD will begin to respond, and within a few days he will be walking politely beside you without pulling on the leash. At first, the training sessions should be kept short and very positive; soon your German Shepherd Dog will be able to walk nicely with you for increasingly longer distances. Remember to give your German Shepherd free time and the opportunity to run and play when you have finished heel practice.

TRAINING TIPS

If not properly socialized and trained, even a well-bred German Shepherd will exhibit bad behaviors such as jumping up, barking, chasing, chewing and other destructive behaviors. You can prevent these habits and help your GSD become the perfect dog you've wished for by following some basic training and behavior guidelines.

Be consistent. Consistency is important, not just in terms of what you allow your GSD to do (get on the sofa, perhaps) and not do (jump up on people), but also in the verbal and body language cues you use with your dog and in his daily routine.

Be gentle but firm. Positive training methods are very popular. Properly applied, dog-friendly methods are wonderfully

Did You Know?

Once your GSD understands what behavior goes with a specific cue, it is time to start weaning her off the food treats. At first, give a treat after each exercise. Then, start to give a treat only after every other exercise. Mix up times when you offer a food reward and when you only offer praise. This way your dog will never know when she is going to receive food and praise, or only praise.

Nobody said that training has to be boring. Make sessions fun by using treats, toys and praise.

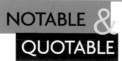

If you want to make your dog happy, create a digging spot where she's allowed to disrupt the earth. Encourage her to dig there by burying bones and toys, and helping her dig them up. — Pat Miller, a certified dog trainer and owner of Peaceable Paws dog-training facility in Hagerstown, Md.

Some German Shepherd Dogs take their training to advanced levels, like working as police K9s!

effective, creating canine–human relationships based on respect and cooperation.

Manage behavior. All living things repeat behaviors that are rewarded. Behaviors that aren't reinforced will go away.

Provide adequate exercise. A tired German Shepherd Dog is a well–behaved German Shepherd Dog. Many behavior problems can be avoided, others resolved, by providing your GSD with enough exercise.

THE THREE-STEP PROGRAM

Perhaps it's too late to give your dog consistency, training and management from the start. Maybe he came from a GSD rescue shelter or you didn't realize the importance of these basic guidelines when he was a puppy. He already may have learned some bad behaviors. Perhaps they're even part of his genetic package. Many problems can be modified with ease using the following three-step process for changing an unwanted behavior.

Step No. 1: Visualize the behavior you want your dog to exhibit. If you simply try to stop your GSD from doing something, you leave a behavior vacuum. You need to fill that vacuum with something, so your dog doesn't return to the same behavior or fill it with one that's even worse! If you're tired of your dog jumping up, decide what you'd prefer instead. A dog who greets people by sitting politely in front of them is a joy to own.

Step No. 2: Prevent your German Shepherd Dog from being rewarded for the behavior you don't want him to exhibit. Management to the rescue! When your GSD jumps up to greet you or get your attention, turn your back and step away to show him that jumping up no longer works in gaining your attention.

Step No. 3: Generously reinforce the desired behavior. Keep in mind that dogs will repeat behaviors that generate rewards. If your GSD no longer gets attention for jumping up and is heavily reinforced with attention and treats for sitting, he will offer sits instead of jumping, because he's learned that sitting will get him what he wants.

COUNTER CONDITIONING

The three-step process helps to correct those behaviors that temporarily gives your GSD satisfaction. For example, he jumps up to get attention; he countersurfs because he finds good food on counters; he nips at your hands to get you to play with him.

The steps don't work well when you're dealing with behaviors that are based in strong emotion, such as aggression and fear, or with hardwired behaviors such as chasing prey. With these, you can change the emotional or hardwired response through counter conditioning — programming a new emotional

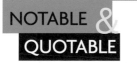

Tell your dog to heel and step out with your left foot. The left leg is the guide for the dog; always start and stop on the left foot. Remember, the idea is to work as a team; this is not a competition between you and your dog.

— Bert A. Haagenstad, a dog trainer and GSD rescuer from Phoenix, Ariz.

SMART TIP!

It's a good idea to enroll your GSD in an obedience class if one is available in your area. Many areas have dog clubs that offer basic obedience training and preparatory classes for obedience competition. There are also local dog trainers who offer similar classes.

or automatic response to the stimulus by giving it a new association. Here's how you would counter condition a GSD who chases after skateboarders while you're walking him on a leash.

1. Have a large supply of high-value treats, such as canned chicken.

2. Station yourself with your GSD on a leash at a location where skateboarders will pass by at a subthreshold distance "X" — that is, where your GSD is alerted to the approaching person but doesn't bark.

3. Wait for a skateboarder. The instant your GSD notices the skateboarder, feed him bits of chicken, nonstop, until the skateboarder is gone. Stop feeding him.

4. Repeat many times until, when the skateboarder appears, your German Shepherd looks at you with a big grin as if to say, "Yay! Where's my chicken?" This is a conditioned emotional response, or CER.

5. When you have a consistent CER at distance X, decrease the distance slightly, perhaps minus 1 foot, and repeat until you consistently get the CER at this distance.

6. Continue decreasing the distance and obtaining a CER at each level, until a skateboarder zooming right past your GSD elicits the "Where's my chicken?" response. Now go back to distance X and add a second skateboarder. Continue this process of desensitization until your GSD doesn't turn a hair at a bevy of skateboarders.

LEAVE IT ALONE

German Shepherds enjoy eating, which makes it easy to train them using treats. But there's a downside to their gastronomic gusto — some GSDs will gobble down anything even remotely edible. This could include fresh food, rotten food, things that once were food and any item that's ever been in contact with food. So, if you don't want your GSD gulping trash, teach him to leave things alone when told.

Place a tempting tidbit on the floor and cover it with your hand (gloved against teeth, if necessary). Say your cue word ("leave it" or "nah"). Your dog might lick, nibble and paw your hand; don't give in or you'll be rewarding bad manners.

Wait until he moves away, then click or praise, and give a treat. Do not let your dog eat the food that's on the floor, only the treats you give him. Repeat until your GSD stops moving toward the tempting food.

Lift your hand momentarily, letting your dog see the temptation. Say the cue word. Be ready to protect the treat but instantly reward him if he resists temptation. Repeat, moving your hand farther away and waiting longer before clicking and rewarding.

Increase the difficulty gradually — practice in different locations, add new temptations, drop treats from standing height, drop several at a time and step away.

Remember to use your cue word, so your dog will know what he's expected to do. Always reward good behavior! Rehearse this skill daily for a week. After that, you'll have enough real-life opportunities to practice.

Training doesn't end once you've mastered the basics. Help your German Shepherd Dog impress your friends with easy tricks.

Even the best dogs have some bad habits. If you are frustrated with a particular behavior that your GSD exhibits, don't despair! Go online and join Club GSD, where you can ask other GSD owners for advice on dealing with excessive digging, stubbornness, housetraining issues and more. Log on to **DogChannel.com/Club-GSD** and click on "Community."

JOIN OUR ONLINE **Club GSD**®

Discipline — training one to act in accordance with rules — brings order to life. It is as simple as that. Without discipline, particularly in a group society, chaos reigns supreme and the group will eventually perish. Humans and canines are social animals and need some form of discipline in order to function effectively. Dogs need discipline in their lives in order to understand how their pack (you and other family members) functions and how they must act in order to survive.

Living with an untrained German Shepherd is a lot like owning a piano that you do not know how to play; it is a nice object to look at but it does not do much more than that to bring you pleasure. Now, try taking piano lessons and suddenly the piano comes alive and brings forth magical sounds and rhythms that set your heart singing and your body swaying.

The same is true of your German Shepherd Dog. Every dog is a big responsibility, and if not sensibly trained may develop

Did You Know?

Anxiety can make a pup miserable. Living in a world with scary, monsters and suspected GSD-eaters roaming the streets has to be pretty nerve-wracking. The good news is that timid dogs are not doomed to be forever ruled by fear. Owners who understand a timid German Shepherd Dog's needs can help her build self-confidence and a more optimistic view of life.

Correctly socializing a German Shepherd puppy will make him a more well-adjusted adult, who will not become startled by new situations and people.

unacceptable behaviors that annoy you or cause family friction.

To train your GSD, you can enroll in an obedience class to teach him good manners as you learn how and why he behaves the way he does. You will also find out how to communicate with your GSD and how to recognize and understand his communications with you. Suddenly your dog takes on a new role in your life; he is interesting, smart, well-behaved and fun to be with. He demonstrates his bond of devotion to you daily. In other words, your German Shepherd Dog does wonders for your ego because he constantly reminds you that you are not only his leader, you are his hero!

Those involved with teaching dog obedience and counseling owners about their dogs' behavior have discovered interesting facts about dog ownership. For example, training dogs when they are puppies results in the highest success rate in developing

NOTABLE & QUOTABLE

The best way to get through to dogs is through their stomach and mind — not the use of force. You have to play a mind game with them.

— *Sara Gregware, a professional dog handler and trainer in Goshen, Conn.*

well-mannered and well-adjusted adult. Training an older German Shepherd, from 6 months to 6 years, can produce almost equal results, providing that the owner accepts the dog's slower learning rate and is willing to patiently work to help him succeed. Unfortunately, many owners of untrained adult dogs lack the patience necessary, so they do not persist until their dogs are successful at learning particular behaviors.

Training a 10- to 16-week-old GSD pup (20 weeks maximum) is like working with a dry sponge in a pool of water. The pup soaks up whatever you teach him and constantly looks for more to do and learn. At this early age, his body is not yet producing hormones, and therein lies the reason for such a high success rate. Without hormones, he is focused on you and is not particularly interested in investigating other places, dogs, people, etc.

You are his leader; his provider of food, water, shelter and security. Your GSD latches onto you and wants to stay close. He will usually follow you from room to room, won't let you out of his sight when you are outdoors with him and will respond in like manner to the people and animals you encounter. If you greet a friend warmly, he will happily greet the person as well. If, however, you are hesitant, even anxious, about the approaching stranger, he will also respond accordingly.

Once your puppy begins to produce hormones, his natural curiosity emerges and he begins to investigate the world around him. It is at this time when you may notice your untrained dog begins to wander away and ignore your cues to stay close.

There are usually training classes within a reasonable distance of your home, but you also can do a lot to train your dog yourself.

The golden rule of dog training is simple. For each "question" (cue), there is only one correct answer (reaction). One cue equals one reaction. Keep practicing the cue until the dog reacts correctly without hesitation. Be repetitive but not monotonous. Dogs get bored just as people do; a bored dog's attention will not be focused on the lesson.

Puppies don't realize that MP3 players aren't for chewing. It's your responsibility to keep your valuable items out of his reach.

Sometimes classes are available but the tuition is too costly, whatever the circumstances, information about training your German Shepherd Dog without formal obedience classes lies within the pages of this book. If the recommended procedures are followed faithfully, you can expect positive results that will prove rewarding for both you and your dog.

Whether your new German Shepherd is a puppy or a mature adult, the teaching methods and training techniques used in basic behaviors are the same. No dog, whether puppy or adult, likes harsh or inhumane training methods. All creatures, however, respond favorably to gentle motivational methods and sincere praise and encouragement.

The following behavioral issues are those most commonly encountered. Remember, every dog and situation is unique. Because behavioral abnormalities are the leading reason for owners' abandoning their pets, we hope that you will make a valiant effort to solve your German Shepherd Dog's behavioral issues.

NIP NIPPING

As puppies start to teethe, they feel the need to sink their teeth into anything — unfortunately that includes your fingers, arms, hair, toes, whatever happens to be available. You may find this behavior cute for about the first five seconds — until you feel just how sharp those puppy teeth are.

Nipping is something you want to discourage immediately and consistently with a firm "No!" (or whatever number of firm "nos" it takes for your dog to understand that you mean business) and replace your finger with an appropriate chew toy.

Did You Know?

Dogs do not understand our language. They can be trained, however, to react to a certain sound, at a certain volume. Never use your German Shepherd's name during a reprimand, as she might come to associate it with a bad thing!

STOP THAT WHINING

A puppy will often cry, whine, whimper, howl or make some type of commotion when he is left alone. This is basically his way of calling out for attention, of calling out to make sure that you know he is there and that you have not forgotten about him. He feels insecure when he is left alone; for example, when you are out of the house and he is in his crate, or when you are in another part of the house and he cannot see you.

The noise he is making is an expression of the anxiety he feels at being alone, so he needs to be taught that being alone is OK. You are not actually training your German Shepherd to stop making noise, you are training him to feel comfortable when he is alone and thus removing the need to make the noise.

This is where his crate with a cozy blanket and a toy comes in handy. You want to know that your pup is safe when you are not there to supervise, and you know he will be in his crate rather than roaming about the house. In order for your pup to stay in his crate without making a fuss, he needs to be comfortable there. On that note, it is extremely important that the crate is never used as a form of punishment, or your GSD puppy will have a negative association with his crate.

Accustom your puppy to his crate in short, gradually increasing time intervals. During these periods, put him in the crate, maybe with a treat, and stay in the room with him. If he cries or makes a fuss, do not go to him, but stay in his sight. Gradually, he will realize staying in his crate is all right without your help and it will not be so traumatic for him when you are not around. You may want to leave the radio on softly when you leave the house; the sound of human voices can comfort him.

Your GSD may howl, whine or otherwise vocalize her displeasure at your leaving the house and her being left alone. This is a normal case of separation anxiety, but there are things that can be done to eliminate this problem. Your dog needs to learn that she will be fine on her own for a while and that she will not wither away if she isn't attended to every minute of the day.

In fact, constant attention can lead to separation anxiety in the first place. If you are endlessly coddling and cuddling your German Shepherd Dog, she will come to expect this from you all of the time, and it will be more traumatic for her when you are not there.

To help minimize separation anxiety, make your entrances and exits as low-key as possible. Do not give your GSD a long, drawn-out good-bye, and do not lavish her with hugs and kisses when you return. This will only make her miss you more when you are away. Another thing you can try is to give your dog a treat when you leave; this will keep her occupied, her mind off the fact that you just left and help her associate your leaving with a pleasant experience.

You may have to acclimate your GSD to being left alone in intervals, much like when you introduced her to her crate. Of course, when your dog starts whimpering as you approach the door, your first instinct will be to run to her and comfort her, but don't do it! Eventually, she will adjust and be just fine — if you take it in small steps. Her anxiety stems from being placed in an unfamiliar situation; by familiarizing her with being alone, she will learn that she will be just fine.

When your German Shepherd is alone in the house, confine her in her crate or a designated dog-proof area. This should be the area in which she sleeps, so she will already feel comfortable there and this should make her feel more at ease when she is alone. This is just one of the many examples in which a crate is an invaluable tool for you and your German Shepherd Dog, and another reinforcement of why your dog should view her crate as a happy place of her own.

CHEW ON THIS

The national canine pastime is chewing! Every dog loves to sink his "canines" into a tasty bone, but anything will do! Dogs chew to massage their gums, make their new teeth feel better and exercise their jaws. This is a natural behavior deeply imbedded in all things canine. Owners should not stop their dog's chewing, but redirect it to chew-worthy objects. A smart owner will purchase proper chew toys for their German Shepherd Dog, like strong nylon bones made for large dogs. Be sure that these devices are safe and durable because your dog's safety is at risk.

The best solution is prevention: That is, put your shoes, handbags and other alluring objects in their proper places (out of the reach of the growing canine mouth). Direct puppies to their toys whenever you see them tasting the furniture legs or the leg of your pants. Make a loud noise to attract your German Shepherd pup's attention and immediately escort him to his chew toy and engage him with the toy for at least four minutes, praising and encouraging him all the while.

NO MORE JUMPING

Jumping is a dog's friendly way of saying hello! Some owners don't mind when their dog jumps, which is fine for them. The problem arises when guests arrive and the dog greets them in the same manner — whether they like it or not! However friendly the greeting may be, chances are your visitors will not appreciate your dog's enthusiasm. Your dog will not be able to distinguish upon whom he can jump and whom he cannot. Therefore, it is probably best to discourage this behavior entirely.

Pick a cue such as "off" (avoid using "down" because you will use that for your dog to lie down) and tell him "off" when he jumps. Place him on the ground on all fours and have him sit, praising him the whole time. Always lavish him with praise and petting when he is in the sit position, that way you are still giving him a warm, affectionate greeting, because you are as pleased to see him as he is to see you!

UNWANTED BARKING MUST GO

Barking is how dogs talk. It can be somewhat frustrating because it is not easy to tell what your dog means by his bark: is he excited, happy, frightened, angry? Whatever it is your dog is trying to say, he should not be punished for barking. It is only when barking becomes excessive, and when excessive barking becomes a bad habit, that the behavior needs to be modified.

If an intruder came into your home in the middle of the night and your dog barked a warning, wouldn't you be pleased? You would probably deem your dog a hero, a wonderful guardian and protector of the home. On the other hand, if a friend unexpectedly drops by, rings the doorbell and is greeted with a sudden sharp bark, you would probably be annoyed at your dog. But isn't it the same behavior? Your dog doesn't know any better ... unless he sees who is at the door and it is someone he is familiar with, he will bark as a means of vocalizing that his (and your) territory is being threat-

SMART TIP!

Do not carry your puppy to her potty area. Lead her there on a leash or, better yet, encourage her to follow you to the spot. If you start carrying her, you might end up doing this routine for a long time, and your puppy will have the satisfaction of having trained you.

NOTABLE & QUOTABLE *Stage false departures. Pick up your car keys and put on your coat, then put them away and go about your routine. Do this several times a day, ignoring your dog while you do it. Soon, her reaction to these triggers will decrease.*

— September Morn, a dog trainer and behavior specialist in Bellingham, Wash.

ened. While your friend is not posing a threat, it is all the same to your dog. Barking is his means of letting you know there is an intruder, whether friend or foe, on your property. This type of barking is instinctive and should not be discouraged.

Excessive, habitual barking, however, is a problem that should be corrected early on. As your German Shepherd Dog grows up, you will be able to tell when his barking is purposeful and when it is for no reason, you will able to distinguish your dog's different barks and with what they are associated. For example, the bark when someone comes to the door will be different from the bark when he is excited to see you. It is similar to a person's tone of voice, except that your GSD has to completely rely on tone because he does not have the benefit of using words. An incessant barker will be evident at an early age.

There are some things that encourage barking. For example, if your dog barks nonstop for a few minutes and you give him a treat to quiet him, he believes you are rewarding him for barking. He will now

Sufficient exercise and outdoor play will keep a GSD happy and tired — and less likely to do bad things due to boredom.

associate barking with getting a treat, and will keep barking until he receives his reward.

FOOD STEALING AND BEGGING

Is your German Shepherd Dog devising ways of stealing food from your cupboards? If so, you must answer the following questions: Is your dog really hungry? Why is there food on the coffee table? Face it, some dogs are more food-motivated than others; some are totally obsessed by a slab of brisket and can only think of their next meal. Food stealing is terrific fun and always yields a great reward — food, glorious food!

Therefore, the owner's goal is to make the reward less rewarding, even startling! Plant a shaker can (an empty can with a lid and filled with coins) on the table so that it catches your pooch off-guard. There are other devices available that will surprise your dog when he is looking for a mid-afternoon snack. Such remote-control devices, though not the first choice of some trainers, allow the correction to come from the object instead of you. These devices are also useful to keep your snacking GSD from napping on forbidden furniture.

Just like food stealing, begging is a favorite pastime of hungry pups with the same reward — food! Dogs learn quickly that humans love that feed-me pose and that their owners keep the good food for themselves. Why would humans dine on kibble when they can cook up sausages and kielbasa? Begging is a conditioned response related to a specific stimulus, time and place; the sounds of the kitchen, cans and bottles opening, crinkling bags and the smell of food preparation will excite your chowhound and soon his paws are in the air!

Here is how to stop this behavior: Never give in to a beggar, no matter how appeal-

ing or desperate! By giving in, you are rewarding your dog for jumping up, whining and rubbing his nose into you. By ignoring your dog, you eventually will force the behavior into extinction. Note that his behavior likely gets worse before it disappears, so be sure there are not any "softies" in the family who will give in to your German Shepherd Dog every time he whimpers "Please."

DIG THIS

Digging, seen as a destructive behavior by humans, is actually quite a natural behavior in dogs. Their desire to dig can be irrepressible and most frustrating. When digging happens, it is an innate behavior redirected into something the dog can do in his everyday life. In the wild, a dog would be actively seeking food, making his own shelter, etc. He would be using his paws in a purposeful manner for his survival. Because you provide him with food and shelter, he has no need to use his paws for these purposes and so the energy he would be using may manifest itself in the form of holes all over your yard and flower beds.

Perhaps your dog is digging as a reaction to boredom — it is somewhat similar to someone eating a whole bag of chips in front of the TV — because they are there and there is nothing better to do! Basically, the answer is to provide your dog with adequate play and exercise so his mind and paws are occupied, and so he feels as if he is doing something useful.

Of course, digging is easiest to control if it is stopped as soon as possible, but it is often hard to catch your dog in the act. If your German Shepherd Dog is a compulsive digger and is not easily distracted by other activities, you can designate an area on your property where it is OK for him to dig. If you catch him digging in an off-limits area of the yard, immediately bring him to the approved area and praise him for digging there. Keep a close eye on him so you can catch him in the act — that is the only way to make him understand where digging is permitted and where it is not. If you take him to a hole he dug an hour ago and tell him "no," he will understand that you are not fond of holes, dirt or flowers. If you catch him while he is stifle-deep in your tulips, that is when he will get your message.

POOP ALERT!

Humans find feces eating, aka *coprophagia*, one of the most disgusting behaviors that their dog could engage in; yet to your dog it is perfectly normal. Vets have found that diets with low digestibility, containing relatively low levels of fiber and high levels of starch, increase *coprophagia*. Therefore, high-fiber diets may decrease the likelihood of your dog eating feces. To discourage this behavior, feed nutritionally complete food in the proper amount. If changes in his diet do not seem to work, and no medical cause can be found, you will have to modify his behavior through environmental control before it becomes a habit.

There are some tricks you can try, such as adding an unpleasant-tasting substance to the feces to make them unpalatable or adding something to your dog's food which will make it unpleasant tasting after it passes through your dog. The best way to prevent your dog from eating his stool is to make it unavailable — clean up after he eliminates and remove any stool from the yard. If it is not there, he cannot eat it.

Never reprimand your dog for stool eating, as this rarely impresses your dog. Vets recommend distracting your German Shepherd while he is in the act. Another option is to muzzle your dog when he goes in the yard to relieve himself; this usually is effective within

30 to 60 days. *Coprophagia* is mostly seen in pups 6 to 12 months, and usually disappears around the dog's first birthday.

AGGRESSION

Aggression, when not controlled, always becomes dangerous. An aggressive German Shepherd, no matter the size, may lunge at, bite or even attack a person or another dog. Aggressive behavior is not to be tolerated. It is more than just inappropriate behavior; it is not safe. It is painful for a family to watch their dog become unpredictable in his behavior to the point where they are afraid of him. While not all aggressive behavior is dangerous, growling and baring teeth can be frightening. It is important to ascertain why your dog is acting in this manner. Aggression is a display of dominance, and your dog should not have the dominant role in his pack, which is, in this case, your family.

It is important not to challenge an aggressive dog, as this could provoke an attack. Observe your German Shepherd Dog's body language. Does he make direct eye contact and stare? Does he try to make himself as large as possible: ears pricked, chest out, neck arched? Height and size signify authority in a dog pack — being taller or "above" another dog literally means that he is "above" in the social status. These body signals tell you that your German Shepherd Dog thinks he is in charge, a problem that needs to be addressed. An aggressive dog is unpredictable: You never know when he is going to strike and what he is going to do. You cannot understand why a dog that is playful and loving one minute is growling and snapping the next.

The best solution is to consult a behavioral specialist, one who has experience with German Shepherd Dogs if possible. Together, perhaps you can pinpoint the cause of your dog's aggression and do something about it. An aggressive dog cannot be trusted and a dog who cannot be trusted is not safe to have as a family pet. If, very unusually, you find that your dog has become untrustworthy and you feel it necessary to seek a new home with a more suitable family and environment, explain fully to the new owners all your reasons for rehoming the dog to be fair to all concerned. In the very worst case, you will have to consider euthanasia.

AGGRESSION TOWARD DOGS

A dog's aggressive behavior toward another dog sometimes stems from insufficient exposure to other dogs at an early age. In German Shepherd Dogs, early socialization with other dogs is essential.

It is the breeder and owner's responsibility to curb and redirect any signs of aggression so that your German Shepherd can become an upright member of canine society. If other dogs make your GSD nervous and agitated, he might use aggression as a defensive mechanism. A dog who has not received sufficient exposure to other canines tends to believe he is the only dog on the planet. He becomes so dominant that he does not even show signs that he is fearful or threatened. Without growling or any other physical signal as a warning, he

NOTABLE & QUOTABLE *The purpose of puppy classes is for puppies to learn how to learn. The pups get the training along the way, but the training is almost secondary.*
— professional trainer Peggy Shunick Duezabou of Helena, Mont.

will lunge at and bite another dog. A way to correct this is to let your German Shepherd Dog approach another dog only when walking on a leash. Watch very closely and at the very first sign of aggression, correct your dog and pull him away. Scold him for any sign of discomfort, and praise him when he ignores or tolerates the other dog. Keep this up until he stops the aggressive behavior, learns to ignore other dogs or accepts other dogs. Praise him lavishly for his correct behavior.

DOMINANT AGGRESSION

A social hierarchy is firmly established in a wild dog pack; dogs want to dominate those under him and please those above him. They know there must be a leader. If you are not the obvious choice for emperor, your dog will assume the throne! These conflicting, innate desires are what you are up against when training your dog. In training a dog to obey cues, you are reinforcing the fact that you are the top dog in the "pack" and that your dog should, and should want to, serve his superior. Thus, you are suppressing your dog's urge to dominate by modifying his behavior and making him obedient.

An important part of training is taking every opportunity to reinforce that you are the leader. The simple action of making your German Shepherd Dog sit to wait for his food says you control when he eats and that he is dependent on you for food. Although it may be difficult, do not give in to your dog's wishes every time he whines at you or looks at you with his pleading eyes. It is a constant effort to show your dog that his place in the pack is at the bottom. This is not meant to sound cruel or inhumane. You love your GSD and you should treat him with care and affection. You cer-

tainly did not get a dog just so you could boss around another creature. Dog training is not about being cruel or feeling important, it is about molding your dog's behavior into what is acceptable and teaching him to live by your rules. In theory, it is quite simple: catch him in appropriate behavior and reward him for it. Add a dog into the equation and it becomes a bit more trying, but as a rule of thumb, positive reinforcement works best.

With a dominant dog, punishment and negative reinforcement can have the opposite effect of what you are trying to achieve. It can make your dog fearful and/ or act out aggressively if he feels he is being challenged. Remember, a dominant dog perceives himself at the top of the social heap and will fight to defend his perceived status. The best way to prevent that is to never give him reason to think he is in control in the first place. If you are having trouble training your German Shepherd Dog and it seems as if he is constantly challenging your authority, seek the help of an obedience trainer or behavioral specialist. A professional will work with both you and your dog to teach you effective techniques to use at home. Beware of trainers who rely on excessively harsh methods; scolding is necessary now and then, but the focus in your training should always be positive reinforcement.

If you can isolate what brings out your GSD's fear reaction, you can help him get over it. Supervise your German Shepherd's interactions with people and other dogs, and praise him when it goes well. If he starts to act aggressively in a situation, correct him and remove him from the situation. Do not let people approach your dog and start petting him without your expressed permission. That way, you can have your dog sit to accept petting and praise him when he behaves appropriately; you are focusing on praise and modifying his behavior by rewarding him. By being gentle and by supervising his interactions, you are showing him that there is no need to be afraid or defensive.

SEXUAL BEHAVIOR

Dogs exhibit certain sexual behaviors that may have influenced your choice of male or female when you first purchased your German Shepherd Dog. To a certain extent, spaying/neutering will eliminate these behaviors, but if you are purchasing a dog that you wish to breed, you should be aware of what you will have to deal with throughout your dog's life.

Female dogs usually have two estruses per year with each season lasting about three weeks. These are the only times in which a female dog will mate, and she usually will not allow this until the second week of the cycle, but this does vary from female to female. If not bred during the heat cycle, it is not uncommon for a female to experience a false pregnancy, in which her mammary glands swell and she exhibits maternal tendencies toward toys or other objects.

Smart German Shepherd Dog owners must also recognize that mounting is not merely a sexual expression. It is also one of dominance. Be consistent and persistent in your training, and you will find that you can move a mounter.

Don't roughhouse with your dog; he'll come to think it is the correct way to play.

FOR THE FUN

One of the best ways to nurture a cooperative and solid relationship with your German Shepherd Dog is to become involved in an activity both of you can enjoy. A bored GSD can easily become a troublesome dog.

Deciding what recreation you and your GSD would enjoy the most takes some consideration. Do you want a sport, such as agility, where you and your dog are both active participants? Would you prefer an activity, such as flyball, where your dog does most of the running? Does something less physical, such as visiting senior citizens, sound more like your cup of tea? Perhaps a brief synopsis of some of the more popular dog-friendly recreations will help you narrow down the choices.

EXERCISE OPTIONS

All German Shepherd Dogs need exercise to keep them physically and mentally healthy. An inactive dog is an overweight dog, who will likely suffer joint strain or torn ligaments. Inactive dogs also are prone to mischief and may do anything to relieve their boredom. This often leads to behavioral problems, such as chewing or barking. Regular daily exercise, such as walks and play sessions, will keep your GSD slim, trim and happy.

Did You Know? The Fédération Internationale Cynologique is the world kennel club that governs dog shows in Europe and elsewhere around the world.

SMART TIP!

Provide your German Shepherd Dog with interactive play that stimulates his mind as well as his body. It's a good idea to have a daily period of one-on-one play, especially with a puppy or young dog. Continue this type of interaction throughout your dog's life, and you will build a lasting bond. Even senior German Shepherds need the stimulation that activity provides.

If your GSD is older or overweight, consult your veterinarian about how much and what type of exercise he needs. Usually, a 10- to 15-minute walk once a day is a good start. As the pounds start to drop off, your dog's energy level will rise, and you can increase the amount of daily exercise.

Whether a dog is trained in the structured environment of a class or alone with his owner at home, there also are many sporting activities that can bring fun and rewards to the owner and his dog once they have achieved basic control.

SCHUTZHUND

Originating in Germany, the sport of schutzhund involves three aspects of training: obedience, tracking and protection. The obedience and tracking portions are difficult enough, but without a doubt what truly sets schutzhund work apart from other competi-

Schutzhund can look violent to an outsider, but it is actually a sport of ultimate control. The popular German dog sport involves three aspects of training: obedience, tracking and protection. Is your German Shepherd up for the challenge?

German Shepherd Dogs don't have to start out loving to fetch. Many of the best flyball dogs love to run and love to tug, which is a reward when they bring back the ball. They start out running for the reward and end up loving to race.

— trainer and flyball enthusiast Regina Steiner of Somerset, N.J.

tive events is the protection phase. In protection work, the dog is taught to bite a human only on a cue from his handler or in the event that he or his handler is attacked. The dog is required to respond to an "out" cue and immediately let go of the individual being bitten. A large dog has enough jaw pressure to actually break an unprotected arm, a sobering fact that illustrates the dedication required of the owner of a protection-trained dog. Unfortunately, schutzhund is perceived to be a sport that makes dogs "mean." In truth, the dog plays an advanced version of tug with special pillows, and later, sleeves worn by a helper. "Schutzhund is a sport, a game where the dog wants to win his prize — not hurt someone," explains top-level competitor Julia Priest of Galt, Calif. However, the amount of training necessary for the three phases requires considerable dedication. "It's time and labor intensive, takes place outdoors in all kinds of weather and requires stamina," Priest says.

To find locations for various training clubs, check out the United Schutzhund Clubs of America website at www.germanshepherd dog.com. The organization allows other breeds to compete but focuses mainly on the GSD. Another option would be DVG America, www.dvgamerica.com, an all-breed association that performs the same training.

Schutzhund provides a fun, exciting and challenging endeavor that is, indeed, fascinating to watch but is even more fascinating to train, as you truly discover what your German Shepherd is all about.

HERDING HAPPINESS

Get your GSD involved in the art of herding. Unlike the Border Collie who gathers wandering sheep from the countryside, the GSD works to keep a flock of 100 to 1,000 sheep within certain boundaries, out of harm's way. When the breed was developed, roadside grazing was common, often relatively close to farmer's crops. "The German Shepherd's original job was to keep the sheep off the road and out of the valuable planted fields," explains Kelly Malone, a herding handler from Ashley, Ohio.

However, before you rush out and buy some sheep, Malone offers this bit of caution. "Just because your dog is a herding breed doesn't mean your individual dog has the right stuff," she says. "To find out if your

GSD has herding instincts, have him evaluated by someone proficient in herding, preferably a person who understands the German Shepherd."

To that end, the German Shepherd Dog Club of America offers a herding instinct test every year at their national specialty (see the website, www.gsdca.org, for the date and location). Additionally, the American Herding Breeds Association and the American Kennel Club also provide testing. Still, Malone feels nothing beats one-on-one time with a private trainer who's knowledgeable and comfortable working with German Shepherds.

Should your dog demonstrate apt potential, Malone says to be prepared and willing to travel to get involved in herding. Because few of us live next to a sheep farm, particularly one that allows "green" dogs to work the flock, lessons usually necessitate going a fair distance. Some folks drive two or three hours on a regular basis, but fortunately, "Once-a-week lessons are sufficient to helping you and your dog learn," Malone says.

Find a herding instructor through your dog's breeder, or if you belong to a local

German Shepherd Dogs were made — literally — for herding. Today, it is more of a sport, for many people, than a way of life.

German Shepherd or all-breed club, ask fellow members if they have any recommendations. Alternatively, the AHBA has a section on its website (www.ahba-herding.org) that lists training facility locations.

Once you find a qualified instructor, your training begins: You must learn how to relinquish control over to your GSD. Though the handler ultimately decides where the sheep go, it becomes "the dog's job to get them there," Malone says. Trusting your dog to make the decisions and letting his instincts rule prove difficult for many owners who have to make this adjustment.

To develop this trust, you'll learn to anticipate your dog's moves and help him succeed. You'll use a staff or rake to keep him from working in too closely, without hurting his drive or confidence. It takes practice to back the dog off stock without hitting him, falling over a sheep, accidentally smacking the instructor, slipping down in mud or committing some other hazardous mistake.

Your instructor will help you teach basic herding cues, such as "go-bye" or "way to me," which sends your dog around the sheep clockwise and counterclockwise, respectively. "Stop," "steady," "slow" and other verbal cues will all fit into your dog's herding education.

If you find your GSD isn't suited for group activities, once you get your veterinarian's OK and basic obedience training behind you, you and your shepherd can find plenty of opportunities for exercise, training and strengthening the bond between you right in your own backyard.

Herding enthusiasts work despite rain, sleet, mud, snow and all sorts of inclement conditions. What makes it worthwhile to Malone and folks like her? "The close bond that develops between the dog and shepherd. For those of us who seek that, there's nothing like it anywhere else," she says.

AGILITY TRIALS

Agility is one of the most popular dog sports. Training your German Shepherd Dog in agility will boost his confidence and train his focus on you.

In agility competition, the dog and handler move through a roped-off course, maneuvering through a series of obstacles that include jumps, tunnels, a dog walk, an A-frame, a seesaw, a pause table and weave poles. Dogs who run through a course without refusing any obstacles, going off course or knocking down any bars, all within a set time, get a qualifying score. Dogs with a certain number of qualifying scores in their given division (Novice, Open, Excellent, and Mach, at AKC trials) earn an agility title.

Several different organizations recognize agility events. AKC-sanctioned events are the most common. The United States Dog Agility Association also sanctions agility trials, as does the United Kennel Club. The rules are different for each of these organizations, but the principles are the same.

When your German Shepherd Dog starts his agility training, he will first learn to negotiate each obstacle while on-leash, as you guide him. Eventually, you will steer him through a few obstacles in a row, one after another. Once he catches on that this is how agility works, he can run a short course off-leash. One day, you'll see the light go on in your German Shepherd Dog's eyes as he figures out he should look to you for guidance as he runs through the course. Your job will

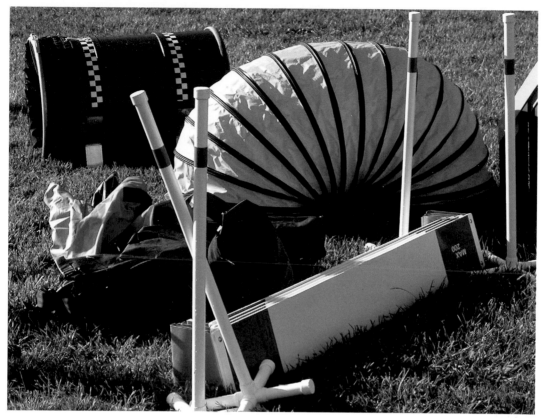

Agility has plenty of fun obstacles — from jumps to tunnels to turns to hoops — that are sure to keep your GSD enthused.

be to tell him which obstacles to take next, using your voice and your body as signals.

OBEDIENCE TRIALS

Obedience trials in the United States trace back to the early 1930s, when organized obedience training was developed to demonstrate how well dogs and their owners could work together. Helen Whitehouse Walke, a Standard Poodle fancier, pioneered obedience trials after she modeled a series of exercises after the Associated Sheep, Police and Army Dog Society of Great Britain. Since Walker initiated the first trials, competitive obedience has grown by leaps and bounds, and today more than 2,000 trials are held in the United States every year, with more than 100,000 dogs competing. Any registered American Kennel Club or United Kennel Club dog can enter an obedi-

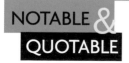

NOTABLE & QUOTABLE *Most dogs in schutzhund were bred from working parents with suitable genetic traits. However, if your GSD will play tug with someone he doesn't know, in a place he's never been before, his prospects are good.*

— top-level schutzhund competitor Julia Priest of Galt, Calif.

Teaching your German Shepherd Dog to watch your every move begins when you first bring her home. Puppies will automatically follow you, even without a leash, because they want to be with you, especially if you have a treat in your hand. Keep your dog on your left side and offer her a small piece of food with each step you take. In no time, your German Shepherd pup will think that you're an automatic treat dispenser, and she will never leave your side.

ence trial for the club in which he is registered, regardless of conformational disqualifications or neutering.

Obedience trials are divided into three levels of progressive difficulty. At the first level, Novice, the dogs compete for the title of Companion Dog; at the intermediate level, Open, dogs compete for a Companion Dog Excellent title; and at the Advanced level, dogs compete for a Utility Dog title. Classes are subdivided into "A" (for beginners) and "B" (for more experienced handlers). A perfect score at any level is 200, and a dog must score 170 or better to earn a "leg," of which three are needed to earn the title. To earn points, the dog must score more than 50 percent of the available points in each exercise; the possible points range from 20 to 40.

Once a dog has earned the Utility Dog title, he can compete with other proven obedience dogs for the coveted title of Utility Dog Excellent, which requires that the dog win "legs" in 10 shows. In 1977, the title Obedience Trial Champion was established by the AKC. Utility Dogs who earn legs in Open B and Utility B earn points toward their Obedience Trial Champion title. To become an OTCh., a dog needs to earn 100 points, which requires three first place wins in Open B and Utility under three different judges.

The Grand Prix of obedience trials, the AKC National Obedience Invitational, gives qualifying Utility Dogs the chance to win the newest and highest title: National Obedience Champion. Only the top 25 ranked obedience dogs, plus any dog ranked in the top three in his breed, are allowed to compete.

RALLY BEHIND RALLY

Rally is a sport that combines competition obedience with elements of agility, but is less demanding than either one of these activities. Rally was designed keeping the average dog owner in mind, and is easier than many other sporting activities.

At a rally event, dogs and handlers are asked to move through 10 to 20 different stations, depending on the level of competition. The stations are marked by numbered signs, which tell the handler the exercise to be performed. The exercises vary from making different types of turns to changing pace.

Dogs can earn rally titles as they get better at the sport and move through the different levels. The titles to strive for are Rally Novice, Rally Advanced, Rally Excellent and Rally Advanced Excellent.

To get your German Shepherd puppy prepared to enter a rally competition, focus on teaching him basic obedience, for starters. Your dog must know the five basic obedience cues — sit, lie down, stay, come and heel — and perform them well. Next, you can enroll your dog in a rally class. Although

More Sports

Thanks to the German Shepherd Dog's multi-tasking skills, there is an entire world of canine sports and activities that awaits you.

DOCKDOGS: A thrilling sport for the water-loving GSD, a dockdog performs a long jump by leaping off a dock of specified proportions to retrieve a toy thrown by her handler. The length of the jump is measured from the edge of the dock to where the dog's rump hits the water, not counting the tail. The Dockdog organization also offers titling.

FLYBALL: Furiously fast, this relay race consists of a box loaded with tennis balls that ejects a ball whenever a dog jumps against the release. Four hurdles, set at a height appropriate for the shortest canine on the team of four, precede the box. Each dog individually leaps across the hurdles, hits the release, catches the ball and repeats her path back to the handler. The North American Flyball Association awards titles and maintains statistics.

BACKPACKING: Backpacking provides an excellent conditioning activity that burns off canine energy while you enjoy a healthy hike. Dogs need properly fitted equipment to prevent discomfort and chafing as they carry water, snacks or their own food for overnight trips. Several organizations offer backpacking titles, including the Dog Scouts of America.

FREESTYLE: Frequently referred to as "dancing with your dog," the harmonious teamwork between owner and dog seen in this sport would dazzle Fred Astaire. Freestyle deftly blends music, dance and dog training into an enjoyable, crowd-pleasing presentation. Individual teams combine traditional obedience moves with leg kicks, swirls, bows and a variety of imaginative moves. The Canine Freestyle Federation and the World Canine Freestyle Organization award titles.

CARTING, SLEDDING, SKIJORING, SCOOTERING: Different approaches to pulling sports than weight pull, each of the aforementioned activities utilize your GSD's pulling strength and are coupled with firm obedience. Carting offers the most likelihood for titling; the rest mainly provide your German Shepherd Dog with great exercise and fun.

he must be at least 6 months of age to compete in rally, you can start training long before his 6-month birthday.

SHOW DOGS

When you purchase your GSD puppy, you must make it clear to the breeder whether you want one just as a lovable companion and pet, or if you hope to purchase a German Shepherd Dog with show prospects. No reputable breeder will sell you a puppy and tell you that he will definitely be show quality because so much can go wrong during the early months of a puppy's development. If you do plan to show, what you hopefully will have acquired is a puppy with show potential.

To the novice, exhibiting a GSD in the ring may look easy, but it takes a lot of hard work and devotion to win at a show such as the annual Westminster Kennel Club Dog Show in New York City, not to mention a fair amount of luck, too!

The first concept that the canine novice learns when watching a dog show is that each dog first competes against members of his own breed. Once the judge has selected the best dog in each breed (Best of Breed) the chosen dog will compete with other dogs in his group. Finally, the dogs chosen first in each group will compete for the Best In Show title.

The second concept you must understand is that the dogs are not actually compared against one another. The judge compares each dog against the breed standard, the written description of the ideal dog approved by the AKC. While some early breed standards were indeed based on specific dogs who were famous or popular, many dedicated enthusiasts say that a perfect specimen as described in the standard has never walked into a show ring, has never been bred and, to the woe of dog breeders around the globe, does not exist. Breeders attempt to get as close to this ideal as possible with every litter, but theoretically the "perfect" dog is so elusive that it is impossible. (And if the perfect dog were born, breeders and judges probably would never agree that he was perfect!)

If you are interested in exploring the world of conformation, your best bet is to join your local breed club or the national (or parent) club, the German Shepherd Dog Club of America. These clubs often host regional and national specialties, shows only for German Shepherd Dogs, which can include conformation as well as obedience and field trials. Even if you have no intention of competing with your German Shepherd Dog, a specialty is like a festival for lovers of the breed who congregate to share their favorite topic: German Shepherd Dogs! Clubs also send out newsletters, and some organize training days and seminars providing owners the opportunity to learn more about their chosen breed. To locate the breed club closest to you, contact the AKC, which furnishes the rules and regulations for all of these events, plus general dog registration and other basic requirements of dog ownership.

CANINE GOOD CITIZEN

If obedience work sounds too regimented but you'd still like your German Shepherd

Dog to have a title, prepare him for the Canine Good Citizen test. This program is sponsored by the AKC, with tests administered by local dog clubs, private trainers and 4-H clubs.

To earn a CGC title, your German Shepherd Dog must be well-groomed and demonstrate the manners that all good dogs should exhibit. The CGC test requires a dog to follow the sit, lie down, stay and come cues, react appropriately to other dogs and distractions, allow a stranger to approach him, sit politely for petting, walk nicely on a loose leash, move through a crowd without going wild, calm down after play or praise, and sit still for an examination by the judge. Rules are posted on the AKC's website.

THERAPY

Visiting nursing homes, hospices and hospitals with your dog can be a tremendously satisfying experience. Many times, a dog can reach an individual who has otherwise withdrawn from the world. The people-oriented German Shepherd Dog can be a delightful therapy dog. Rescue worker Lois Brooks says this breed seems to have an affinity for children that makes it a natural for visiting children in hospitals or mental care facilities. Although a gentle disposition is definitely a plus, the often normally rambunctious dog seems to instinctively become gentler when introduced to those who are weak or ailing. Some basic obedience is, of course, a necessity for the therapy dog and a repertoire of tricks is a definite bonus. The sight of a clownish German Shepherd Dog "hamming it up" can help brighten most anyone's day.

Most facilities require a dog to have certification from a therapy dog organization. Therapy Dog International and the Delta Society are two such organizations. Generally speaking, if your dog can pass a Canine Good Citizen test, earning certification will not be difficult. Certified therapy dog workers frequently get together a group and regularly make visitations in their area.

To find more information about this popular breed, contact the following organizations. They will be glad to help you dig deeper into the world of German Shepherd Dogs.

American German Shepherd Rescue Association. This organization offers rescue support information. www.agsra.com

American Herding Breed Association: Herding is great for shepherds; it's what they were bred to do. www.ahba-herding.org

American Kennel Club: The AKC website offers information and links to conformation, tracking, rally, obedience and agility programs, and member clubs. www.akc.org

Canadian Kennel Club: Our northern neighbor's oldest kennel club is similar to the AKC in the states. www.ckc.ca

Canine Performance Events: Sports for dogs to keep them active. www.k9cpe.com

Dog Scouts of America: Take your dog to camp. www.dogscouts.com

DVGAmerica: Your GSD can channel his energy and build some muscle by participating in schutzhund. www.dvgamerica.com

Love on a Leash: Your GSD has a lot of love to give. www.loveonaleash.org

it's a **Fact**

The **American Kennel Club** was established in 1884. It is America's oldest kennel club. The **United Kennel Club** is the second oldest in the United States and began registering dogs in 1898.

National Association of Professional Pet Sitters: Hire someone to watch your dog. www.petssitters.org

North American Dog Agility Council: This site provides links to clubs, obedience trainers and agility trainers in the United States and Canada. www.nadac.com

Therapy Dogs Inc.: Get your GSD involved in therapy. www.therapydogs.com

Therapy Dogs International: Find more therapy dog info here: www.tdi-dog.org

United Kennel Club: The UKC offers several of the events offered by the AKC, including agility, conformation and obedience. In addition, the UKC offers competitions in hunting and dog sport (companion and protective events). Both the UKC and the AKC offer programs for junior handlers, ages 2 to 18. www.ukcdogs.com

United Schutzhund Clubs of America: More schutzhund information can be found here. www.germanshepherddog.com

United States Dog Agility Association: The USDAA has information on training, clubs and events in the United States, Canada, Mexico, and overseas. www.usdaa.com

World Canine Freestyle Organization: Dancing with your dog is fun! www.world caninefreestyle.org

Don't let your GSD s-i-t all day. Get involved in a dog sport.

Plan your vacation to include your dog. However, if your destination isn't Fido-friendly, have a good boarding place already lined up.

BOARDING

So you want to take a family vacation — and you want to include all members of the family. You usually make arrangements for accommodations ahead of time anyway, but this is imperative when traveling with a dog. You do not want to make an overnight stop at the only place around for miles only to discover that the hotel doesn't allow dogs. Also, you don't want to reserve a room for your family without confirming that you are traveling with a GSD because if it is against the hotel's policy, you may not have a place to stay.

Alternatively, if you are traveling and choose not to bring your GSD, you will have to make arrangements for him. Some options are to leave him with a family member or a neighbor, have a trusted friend stop by often or stay at your house. Another option is leaving your GSD at a reputable boarding kennel.

If you choose to board him at a kennel, visit in advance to see the facilities and check how clean they are, and where the dogs are kept. Talk to some of the employees and see how they treat the dogs. Do they spend time with the dogs either during play or exercise? Also, find out the kennel's policy on vaccinations and what they require. This is for all of the dogs' safety because when dogs are kept together, there is a greater risk of diseases being passed between them.

HOME STAFFING

For the German Shepherd Dog parent who works all day, a pet sitter or dog walker may be the perfect solution for the lonely shepherd longing for a midday stroll. Dog owners can approach local high schools or community centers if they don't have a neighbor who is interested in a part-time commitment. Interview potential dog walkers and consider their experience with dogs, as well as your GSD's rapport with the candidate. (German Shepherd Dogs are excellent judges of character.) Always check references before entrusting your dog and opening your home to a new dog walker.

For an owner's long-term absence, such as a business trip or vacation, many German Shepherd Dog owners welcome the services of a pet sitter. It's usually less stressful on the dog to stay home with a pet sitter than to be boarded in a kennel. Pet sitters also may be more affordable than a week's stay at a full-service doggie day care.

Pet sitters must be even more reliable than dog walkers because the dog is depending on his surrogate owner for all of his needs over an extended period. Owners are advised to hire a certified pet sitter through the National Association of Professional Pet Sitters (www.petsitters.org). NAPPS provides online and toll-free pet sit-

ter locator services. The nonprofit organization only certifies serious-minded, professional individuals who are knowledgeable in canine behavior, nutrition, health and safety. Whether or not you take your GSD with you, always keep your German Shepherd Dog's best interest at heart when planning a trip.

SCHOOL'S IN SESSION

Puppy kindergarten, which is usually open to dogs between 3 to 6 months of age, allows puppies to learn and socialize with other dogs and people in a structured setting. Classes helps to socialize your German Shepherd Dog so that he will enjoy going places with you and be a well-behaved member in public gatherings. They prepare him for adult obedience classes and for a lifetime of social experiences he will have with your friends and his furry friends. The problem with most puppy kindergarten classes is that they only occur one night a week.

If you're home during the day, you may be able to find places to take your puppy so he can socialize. Just be careful about dog parks and other places that are open to any dog. An experience with a dog bully can undo all the good your training classes have done.

If you work, your puppy may be home alone all day, a tough situation for a German Shepherd Dog. Chances are he can't hold himself that long, so your potty training will be undermined — unless you're teaching him to use an indoor potty. Also, by the time you come home, he'll be bursting with energy, and you may think that he's hyperactive and uncontrollable.

The only suitable answer for the working professional with a German Shepherd Dog is doggie day care. Most large cities have some sort of day care, whether it's a boarding kennel that keeps your dog in a run or a full-service day care that offers training, play time and even spa facilities. They range from a person who keeps a few dogs at his or her home to a state-of-the-art facility built just for dogs. Many of the more sophisticated doggie day cares offer webcams so you can see what your dog is up to throughout the day. Things to look for:

- escape-proof facilities, such as gates in doorways that lead outside
- inoculation requirements for new dogs
- midday meals for young dogs
- obedience training (if offered), using reward-based methods
- safe and comfortable nap areas
- screening of dogs for aggression
- small groups of similar sizes and ages
- toys and playground equipment, such as tunnels and chutes
- trained staff, with an adequate number to supervise the dogs (no more than 10 to 15 dogs per person)
- a webcam

Remember to keep your dog's leash slack when interacting with other dogs. It is not unusual for a dog to pick out one or two canine neighbors to dislike. If you know there's bad blood, step off to the side and find a barrier, such as a parked car, between the dogs. If there are no barriers to be had, move to the side of the walkway, cue your GSD to sit, stay and watch you until her nemesis passes; then continue your walk.

SMART TIP!

CAR TRAVEL

You should accustom your German Shepherd Dog to riding in a car at an early age. You may or may not take him in the car often, but at the very least he will need to go to the vet once in a while, and you do not want these trips to be traumatic for the dog or troublesome for you. The safest way for a dog to ride in the car is in his crate. If he uses a crate in the house, you can use the same crate for travel.

Another option is a specially made safety harness for dogs, which straps your GSD in the car much like a seat belt would. Do not let the dog roam loose in the vehicle; this is very dangerous! If you should make an

abrupt stop, your dog can be thrown and injured. If your dog starts climbing on you while you are driving, you will not be able to concentrate on the road. It is an unsafe situation for everyone — human and canine.

For long trips, stop often to let your GSD relieve himself. Take along whatever you need to clean up after him, including some paper towel should he have an accident in the car or suffer from motion sickness.

IDENTIFICATION

Your German Shepherd Dog is your valued companion and friend. That is why you always keep a close eye on him, and you have made sure that he cannot escape from the yard or wriggle out of his collar and run away from you. However, accidents can happen and there may come a time when your GSD unexpectedly gets separated from you. If this should occur, the first thing on your mind will be finding him. Proper identification, including an ID tag, a tattoo and possibly a microchip, will increase the chances of his being returned to you safely and quickly.

An ID tag on a collar or harness is the primary means of identifying a lost pet (and ID licenses are required in many cities). Although inexpensive and easy to read, collars and ID tags can come off or be taken off.

A microchip doesn't get lost. The microchip is embedded underneath the dog's skin and contains a unique ID number that is read by scanners. It comes in handy for identifying lost or stolen pets. However, to be effective, the microchip must be registered in a national database. Smart owners will register their dog and regularly check that their contact information is kept up-to-date.

However, one thing to keep in mind is that not every shelter or veterinary clinic has a scanner, nor do most folks who might pick up and try to return a lost pet. Your best best? Get both!

Did You Know?

Some communities have created regular dog runs and separate spaces for small dogs. These small-dog runs are ideal for introducing puppies to the dog park experience. The runs are smaller, the participants are smaller and their owners are often more vigilant because they are used to watching out for their fragile companions.

INDEX

GERMAN SHEPHERD DOG, a Smart Owner's Guide®
part of the Kennel Club Books® Interactive Series®

JOIN Club GSD® TODAY!

LIBRARY OF CONGRESS CATALOGING-IN-PUBLICATION DATA
German shepherd dog / from the editors of Dog fancy magazine.
    p. cm. — (Smart owner's guide)
Includes bibliographical references and index.
ISBN 978-1-59378-755-4
1. German shepherd dog. I. Dog fancy (San Juan Capistrano, Calif.)
SF429.G37G47 2010
636.737'6—dc22

            2009028952